THE
IMPORTANCE
OF BEING
ETON

NICK FRASER

W0010567

THE
IMPORTANCE
OF BEING
ETON

NICK FRASER

✳ SHORT BOOKS

First published in 2006 by
Short Books
3A Exmouth House
Pine Street, London EC1R 0JH

10 9 8 7 6 5 4 3 2 1

PICTURE CREDITS
pgs 12, 39, 61, 100, 152, 177:
Photographs by L. Moholy-Nagy taken from Portrait of Eton (Frederick Muller, 1949)
pgs 113, 208, 220:
Reproduced by kind permission of the Provost and Fellows of Eton College

A CIP catalogue record for this book
is available from the British Library.

ISBN 1-904977-53-7

Printed in Great Britain by
William Clowes Ltd, Beccles, Suffolk

For my mother, who always saved me, and for my daughter Isabelle: 'Never trust an Etonian.'

Top hats left outside the door, 1937

CHAPTER ONE

Eton means many things, both to those who, as it it still said, have 'been' there, and to those, more numerous, who haven't. For myself it spells something distant and hard to recapture. I know that I was educated at Eton but find that, evidence of my presence notwithstanding, it doesn't feel entirely real. Am I looking at myself, or at a cunningly concocted imposture? What did I do there – or, more appropriately, what was done to me? I don't ask such questions frequently, but the question of Eton has come back to me in the oddest places. I wonder how it is possible that on the only two occasions I have worn an O.E. tie (one of them in New York, the other in Cape Town) I should have been asked by someone – in New York, indeed, someone who came up to me in the street – in which 'house' I was. I don't follow Eton around, and Eton certainly doesn't seek after me. But there must be something behind these intermittent, dream-like half-connections. Something of the place must inhabit me, otherwise I wouldn't feel impelled to write about it.

***

I once got a summer job, aged 21, cramming two Etonians in the hope that they would get to university. What attracted me, I suppose, was the exotic aspect of the job – I was to stay on the Balmoral estate, in a house once used by Queen Victoria for her encounters with her favourite gamekeeper. The house was poky and dark, overlooking a stretch of dank moor and a forest. It was now inhabited each summer by Sir Martin Charteris, the Queen's Private Secretary, shortly to be ennobled, and appointed Provost of Eton. My duties weren't excessive. Each day we'd do some history, a little French or a piece of verse:

If ever any beauty I did see,
Which I desired and got, 'twas but a dream of thee

Hal had the angular, pale looks feasted on by generations of portraitists. Clearly, his fate was to be admired. Bulkier, already clubbable, Chas got his way in life by pretending never to have quite understood things. They were intelligent and, as one might expect from Etonians, sure of themselves. 'You really are an Oxford man,' they teased when I tried to teach them anything. In between our studies they talked wistfully about girls, dances, holidays, voicing their own sexual frustrations in rainy Scotland freely. 'I'm sick of wanking,' observed Chas one morning. 'Does one go on wanking all one's life?'

Of course, they talked about what they called 'School', capitalising the word as if there could be no other. Did I know X's cousin, or Y, all good chaps, or Z, a total crasher? Had I been there with Trench-Motter or Dufferin, or Paley, or Cranley-Headstart? C-H had been sent down in mysterious circumstances. ('Well, he just got up to things,' was how Hal described it.) They understood whose parents were rich, and whose were not. They remembered goals scored, drunken binges, bizarre infractions of school dress, just as they were up on details of town houses, country houses, places in the South of France. And they were familiar with the qualities of sisters whom they discussed endlessly, but where these girls were concerned, their observations were remote, tellingly naïve. 'Remember that hat she was wearing at the Fourth of June,' Chas said wistfully about someone's sister: 'Do you think she'll go for me?' 'She might,' said Hal, after due consideration. 'But I bet you won't,' he said. 'You won't even dare.'

Sir Martin was friendly in a busy way, pink and hearty. He disappeared frequently to the large house up the drive, carrying papers, returning preoccupied. Royal moods or doings were discussed sotto voce. I developed a passion for his blond, and beautiful niece, striving without success to break through a wall of shyness in between helpings of cold grouse. While tutoring, I thought of my own education at Eton, and how it appeared to have consisted of waiting for something I could never specify. As one grey day followed another, I began to wonder what it had really given me. In the afternoons we'd drive off in the Private Secretary's mini. Hal wasn't bothered by such small details as bumps and half-tarred shoulders. Nor, it became apparent, were those whom Hal jokingly called Brenda and Phil. On one occasion we avoided their royal Land Rover piloted by the Prince only by veering off-road into a clump of heather.

One day Sir Martin announced over breakfast that we were going to the Servants' Ball. 'You'll enjoy this, Hal said brightly. He explained that I would need a dinner jacket and, since I had none, set about devising an alternative. My black 1960s drainpipe jeans (favoured by Mods, they were rapidly taken up by Etonians, who, when they were interdicted as school wear, inked their striped trousers) would just about do. Hal managed to pin up a jacket of one of his father's dark suits. A spare bow tie was available. I looked terrible, and said so. 'Do I have to go? I asked. 'Actually, you look like an Eton beak', Hal said. 'You'll be fine.'

There were many red-haired girls called Morag or Sandra at the Servants' ball, and they were kitted out in tartan sashes and long dresses, with sprigs of heather. The men were ruddy-faced, bandy-legged in kilts and stockings, with the pained expression that is to be found in devotedly monarchist Scots. I noticed wood panelling, and an acreage of deep-pile, reddish floral carpeting. I explored what appeared to be a museum of the British Ancien Regime. In one room I found portraits of each one of the chief ghillies, with their dogs, dead stags at their feet. I knew, and still know nothing, about Highland dancing; but I joined the Paul Jones, moving hand in hand with a beaming, kilted Prince Philip. When the music stopped, I was aghast to find myself opposite the rotund, outsize china doll figure of the Queen Mother. I am not sure to this day how we got through Strip The Willow, or indeed the Gay Gordons – somehow we did. I had been told that one wasn't supposed to speak to royalty until addressed, so I kept mum. For her part she appeared pleased to find out that I was at Oxford. 'I suppose you went to Eton before that,' she observed, looking me up and down, taking in my makeshift garb with what might have been an approving giggle.

***

Not to hold the English upper classes in very special regard, declining opportunities to dress, eat or speak like them, may not seem so unusual these days. Perhaps my dance floor encounter with the Queen Mother was so bizarre an occurrence that it more than satisfied any social climbing cravings. But I have never wholly exhausted my interest in Eton, which continues to draw me back into the English past. Eton, I suspect, is how I retain a certain knowledge of the arcana of what used to be known as class consciousness – how the smallest gesture or variation of dress code can be said, though this is not always the case, to betray identity. It is still possible to be fascinated by the ways in which English people contrive to separate themselves from each other, constructing new edifices of discrimination even as they tear down the old ones – indeed no-one choosing to live in England, even a hermit or street dweller, could claim to live in ignorance of such things. I think of Eton as a predominantly English institution, fascinating for what it tells about class and power. And I think of it (and Etonians) as displaying most fully, and with very little hypocrisy, the very

English capability of holding on, holding tight indeed, even while appearing to give way. When it comes to understanding such things, I tell myself that I am helped by not really being English, and thus a half-spectator.; but there is a small degree of delusion here. Real Etonians, *real* English people indeed, know these things without feeling that they have to write about them. In the kind of England that Eton represents it isn't necessary to write about the things you really know – because your friends will all share the knowledge anyhow.

And yet the strange Eton aura subsists in the atmosphere, still transforming whatever it touches. I was in Paris meeting a French professor friend the day it became apparent that David Cameron (JF 84, as the Old Etonian Association List Of Members describes him) received enough votes for the Tory leadership run-off. Over lunch, my friend became excited. (Along with the British royal family, mention of Eton is guaranteed to excite the French, provoking a paroxysm of innocent snobbery among *gauchistes* and *la droite traditionelle* alike.) 'Will there really be another Old Etonian running Britain?' he asked.

In a nearby bookstore he directed my attention to a series of lectures entitled *Class Struggle*, given by the liberal *penseur* Raymond Aron in 1956. One chapter was called 'Social Mobility and the Circulation of Elites':

In Britain, at least three different roads lead to a parliamentary career. First, there is the ancient, highly traditional network: a man from the upper class (*la bonne société*), who has been to Eton, Oxford or Cambridge (where he may perhaps have studied Middle Eastern or Far Eastern languages), owns a house in a constituency somewhere in England, where his father, grandfather or uncle were also MPs; he succeeds them, he is elected and reaches some sort of level in the hierarchy of ministers. That is the ideal (and typical) career of a conservative politician.

Plus ça change indeed. Aron, it is clear, approved of such a tradition, contrasting it favourably with the lack of a coherent class in France. (He was writing before French politics were dominated by *énarques* – graduates of the French elite school of public administration, modelled consciously on Oxford and Cambridge, though somewhat different in their attitudes). And he was probably thinking of Anthony Eden, who was Prime Minister when these words were written, and who did study Arabic at Oxford, speaking nearly perfect French, though his brief period in power proved to be disastrous for Anglo-French relations. Otherwise the portrait could be a more recent one.

On the train returning to London, I checked out the *Daily Telegraph* – still, despite a degree of recent slippage, renowned as the Conservative Party's broadsheet. Four separate pieces described aspects of Cameron's Etonianness, ranging from his White's Club membership (approved of) to his penchant for classless leisurewear (viewed as a necessary concession to current middle-class taste). The subject received its fullest treatment in a piece by Charles Moore (former Editor of the *Telegraph*, KS 74) entitled Jolly Voting Weather (of course) and surveying the Eton ethos:

All this can lead to bad things – arrogance, exclusiveness, and unmerited assumption of entitlement, an emotional crutch for the talentless – but not all bad. It would be an exceptionally stupid or nasty Etonian (yes, both species exist) who did not have a strong sense of obligation to his country, a sort of mental map of how our public life worked and some worldly confidence that he could contribute to it... I have never asked David Cameron about any of this, but I would guess from his public demeanour and private attitudes that such feelings are strong in him, and I feel glad about that.

This was the purest Etonspeak – indeed it could have

come straight from the school magazine, the *Eton College Chronicle*. But so, too, could the parody by Craig Brown (GRSt.A 75), of 'Dave' Cameron's Blairish, touchy-feely oration at the Blackpool Conference (he had patted his pregnant wife's bump, and – another miracle for the intelligence-starved Tories – spoken without notes):

Let's have the courage to reconnect with our feelings. But first let us check that they are reconnected with our aspirations, and our aspirations are reconnected with our hopes, and our hopes are reconnected with our feelings. Then, and then only, can we go forward together. What we need now, above all, is a sense of direction. Well, I've got that sense of direction. It's a sense of direction that says: 'Let's go forward with confidence. Because if you don't go forward with confidence, you'll start to wiggle. And then you'll be turning your back on going in a straight line.'

Eton culture – gossipy, half-disrespectful, teasing, packed with in-jokes and more than a little pompous when something as serious as the reputation of the school is at stake – still lives. How could it ever die?

***

The years between the mid-1960s, when I was sent to Eton, and the present, have transformed notions of what is posh in Britain, even while much new wealth, not evenly distributed, has been created. There still appears to be life in the great primary symbol of Britain, which remains the Monarchy. But the power of old money, exemplified by the class of landed aristocracy, has waned; and old centres of prestige such as the Army or the Church are wholly gone. Eton has so far cunningly avoided the fate of its former patrons and clients. But it appears not wholly to have escaped unscathed. Although the school turns away many would-be Etonians, retaining a reputation for classiness as well as high educational standards, its negative cachet is intense – no other 'public school'* is viewed with such envy and reprobation, and no place is so rancorously identified with the survival of privilege. (In some quarters, indeed, not just among tabloid reporters, one might assume that Eton had actually caused, or perpetuated the arrangements of

*The use of the adjectives 'independent' and 'public' in relation to schools that are private has long been a source of confusion, and not just to foreigners. Throughout this book I've chosen to use the term 'public school' in relation to Eton because this is how the school has been referred to for most of its history. It is additionally confusing that Etonians used to refer to 'private school' (as in 'my Private'), but this was when talking about the preparatory school they had attended before Eton.

class, rather than merely, as is perhaps the case, giving expression to them.) And the school, so adept in the practice of politics, has appeared to falter in the face of modernity. It has often seemed both too grand for the present and, by its own often brutally ambitious standards, not quite ruthless enough.

The trouble with Eton is that it compels Britons to ask what they really want from their elite. Is it enough to be rich, or clever, or both – or is one required, once in a while, in the style fatally adopted by the House of Windsor, to display some signs of conspicuous social utility? No-one any more knows the answers to these questions – or indeed bothers to ask them. But they are still important – not just in Britain – and they do lie at the heart of the long story of Eton.

I hope this book won't be seen as an autobiography, or a history, or a piece of reportage, although it contains elements of all three. And I must emphasise, so as not to mislead the unwary, that this is not an act of self-expiation or therapy. Long ago, I feel I understood the part Eton did or didn't play in making me. But I do act as a protagonist as well as a spectator in these pages. To use a metaphor familiar from sporting Eton life, I may sometimes rush onto the pitch while retaining my place on the sidelines. This is because I simply want to say what happened. Most of all I am interested in the growth and decline of prestige, glamour and influence. I wish to describe how it is that one school, with remarkable buildings, a tenacious attachment to an out-of-date dress code, and many arcane social habits, came to find a distinctive place in the national imagination, spreading a vivid, often wholly misleading idea of itself and England throughout the world. I am indeed interested in the importance of being Eton.

CHAPTER TWO

It isn't so difficult to get to Eton – you take the train from London, alighting at Royal Windsor and walk past the blockhouse ugly castle; or you can go by car, leaving the fumes of the M4 via Datchet, passing pubs and small houses. This isn't a spectacular approach.

Just before you arrive it's possible to see, over the wall, the pepperpot spires of College Chapel, and what Anthony Powell, embarking on his novel cycle, called 'tenement-like structures, experiments in architectural insignificance, that intruded upon a central concentration of buildings, commanding and antiquated' – a sentence that appears to mean that, as in much of the rest of England, some of the architecture is alright, but much of it is not.

You can stop, and walk in either direction. On the High

Street, you'll find an old inn, where boys get drunk, and then a number of tailors whose windows are filled with old-fashioned looking clothes, and in which attentive salesmen still sell specimens of the school's 67 sports caps, or school gear. ('We don't do second-hand ones, and recommend against polyester on the ground that it doesn't wear,' the assistant will say, urging you to spend £175 on each suit.) In the other direction you can go into the yard, with its stained statue of the Founder, orb and sceptre raised, and damp, quiet cloisters. You can linger in Chapel, with its war memorials, its carved stalls, its John Piper windows illustrating the Parables and Miracles – the Raising of Lazarus, the Feeding of the Five Thousand, the House on the Sand, the Light Under a Bushel, etc. There are ghostly-grey wall paintings on each side, with faint, elegant figures as languorous as Etonians. These were executed in the 1470s, and painted over by a barber in the Reformation, later covered once again. They were only retrieved from oblivion in the 1920s on the order of the Provost M.R. James, appropriately a ghost story writer. They depict, among other events, the life of the Virgin Mary, to whose memory the school was once dedicated.

In good weather you can go round the back of the Chapel, climb over a stile, crossing a small foot-bridge into a small, exquisitely landscaped area with seats, benches and sundial called Fellow's Eyot. This is said to be where the young Shelley did his homework. Look through the trees here, between a clump of willow and two swans, and you might think yourself in the midst of an eighteenth century pastoral scene, perhaps Thomas Gray's poem about Eton:

Whose turf, whose shade, whose flowers among
Wanders the hoary Thames along
His silver-winding way.

On the way back you can take in the suite of rooms, in which is installed what is called, without apparent irony, The Museum of Eton Life. Here is the flogging block used by the redoubtable Dr. Keate, with a genuine specimen of a birch. And here are numerous blazers, caps, photos of long-gone boys etc.; and, on the far wall, facing a somewhat anodyne contemporary video showing a day at Eton, a *tableau vivant* depicting what the school guide book help-fully calls 'a life-size and authentically recreated senior boy's room of c. 1900':

While the lowly fag prepares toast for his master by the coal fire, the Wall-playing grandee reclines in a chair by his desk, listening to the gossip from his Pop visitor. Around the walls, on the table, desk, mantelpiece and floor lie in disarray all the paraphernalia of a boy's life: the plate from Rowland's (a school tuck shop, now defunct), the discarded Latin exercises, ribboned lists of teams and pictures of Eton in their characteristic Oxford frames.

If you are assiduous, you may want to walk to the Wall itself, where the school competes against itself in a game that is as brutal in appearance as it is difficult to follow. The bricks are worn down by generations of ritual fighting. On St. Andrew's Day, when the School's teams compete, Collegers pitted against Oppidans, boys sit on top of the wall cheering on, or jeering. You can wander on, into the billiard-table playing fields, with exotic names like Agar's or Dutchman's Plough, and back to the sleepy river itself, with its overhang of trees.

In the English style, it doesn't seem grand; nor do the boys themselves, strolling to and from rowing, dressed in old trainers and faded sweatshirts, or slouching to and from work, carrying books. Only the eighteenth century uniforms are immediately astonishing (though the top hats went during the Second World War; as did, in the late 1960s, the celebrated Eton jackets, or 'bumfreezers', worn with a grotesquely high collar, which, to their shame and frustration, were inflicted on small boys) and the bizarre combinations of jackets and striped trousers still worn by those who teach them. You'll notice that many 'beaks', as they are called, still ride old bicycles so slowly that they seem always about to lose their balance. When boys pass a beak they are supposed to raise their hands to a place between forehead and shoulder, as if raising a hat.

***

I went to Eton one late winter day in order to meet the new Head Master. Fiftyish, wearing striped trousers, a black jacket, a white bow tie with a high 'stick-up' collar and steel-rimmed specs, and with a full, greyish head of hair, Anthony Little (I knew he would want to be called Tony) reminded me of many people I had known or even worked for – a senior executive at the BBC, perhaps, or a head of human resources in a progressively-run large company, or even a well-spoken New Labour or Liberal Democrat M.P. There was no whiff of old-style Tory about him, nor did it seem – a habitual trait among posh schoolmasters – as if he might ever have contemplated a career as an Anglican bishop. Educated at Eton, as a chorister (on one of the scholarships awarded for singing voices happily combined with intelligence) he had worked at other private schools, returning just over a year ago.

I'd heard mutterings among boys to the effect that Tony was somehow a lightweight, a choice made on the shallow grounds of presumed acceptability. 'He doesn't teach,' appeared to be a refrain, 'most Head Men have some pretensions to scholarship.' I found him to be sympathetic as well as steely. He didn't believe the school should abandon its antiquated dress, and he speedily rejected any notions of Eton becoming co-educational. It was clear that he had got the job by evoking the Burkean notion (a principle frequently cited by the English elite despite the fact that it has not always been put into practice) that 'a society without change is without the means of its preservation.' Tony pioneered a new 'two-strikes-and-out' policy towards drug offenders. I'd heard that he had both acted in and produced plays, and I noticed that our meeting involved a strong, near-camp element of performance. I might have believed that I was interviewing the headmaster, but it was he who was doing the finding out. No matter what we seemed to talk about, I could sense boxes being ticked. And he wanted to know about journalists. Why was so much reporting ill-informed or misleading? Was the activity of reporting indeed so decayed that one should assume that nothing written on a subject was ever close to the truth?

'Eton is a four letter word,' Tony said. 'When I was at Eton, Eton was called a school for toffs. And it's still called a school for toffs, despite the fact that everybody knows this isn't really true. It's simplistic, it's a caricature, it's non-thinking, it's myth.' For Tony, being Head Master at Eton implied a never-ending, heroic struggle with falsehood. One was required ceaselessly to correct mistaken impressions – about the use of drugs (this had replaced homosexuality as a prime concern, presenting him with the most ticklish disciplinary problems), about price-fixing (a controversy that had arisen recently in relation to collusion allegedly exercised by major public schools). He talked about one scholar culled by Eton from East London, whose tower-block neighbours had spoken to a tabloid paper.

'I suppose they wanted to make money,' he said, 'but it wasn't fair to the boy. Why shouldn't he come to Eton?' Nowadays, he lamented, one had only to type Eton College into Google in order to appreciate that the notoriety of the school meant that stories immediately went around the world. In the midst of the SARS epidemic, rumours had circulated to the effect that Eton boys on a trip abroad, potential carriers of the epidemic, had been excused the normal quarantine measures. He had even received letters suggesting that he and the school should be prosecuted for letting loose a plague on Britain.

The headmaster's study was filled with books, with the appropriate sofas and cut flowers. As a prospective parent, specially a foreign one, it would be easy to conclude, visiting Mr. Little, that the yearly expenditure of £23,000 – there are, to be sure, additional items such as the distinctive clothes, the ambitious holiday ventures sponsored by the school, the expense of staying with rich friends, etc. – was well spent. I imagined that the headmaster took these things for granted. But it was clear that, like so many of his tormentors, he felt uneasy – as if he, too, perhaps wasn't sure that the whole Eton thing could last. The government's notion that universities ought to compensate for the lower results achieved by state schools, by applying what amounted to quotas alarmed him. What was the point of sending your children at such cost to Eton if they were going to be penalised for over-achieving? Although numbers were small, a steadily higher proportion of Etonians were admitted to American universities each year. Did I think that in the future a Labour government might act against private education? Trying to measure worry levels, I concluded that Tony was a serious man. He really did, in an old-fashioned way, see the stewardship of Eton as both a burden and a privilege. Press assaults on Eton threatened what he did as well as offending his sense of fairness.

Evidently, there were benefits, too, in running Eton. From Canton in China a delegation had recently come demanding to know how the ethos of Eton might be adapted for post-Communist China. Did I know that almost 80 boys at Eton were taught Mandarin Chinese? (This was more than twice the number who studied German – the Chinese master, a German by birth, nationality and education, didn't teach German.) Eton didn't believe in franchising, but the Japanese, worried about the decline of traditional values, were shortly to establish a Shinto version of the school. '*Noblesse oblige* sounds good in Japanese,' Tony chuckled, revealing a weakness for schoolmasterly jokes.

***

There are 1290 pupils at Eton, all of them boarders. Formerly 'put down for the school at birth', boys can now be entered as late as ten and a half years old. They are selected by means of the Common Entrance exam, routine among independent, or 'public' schools, and those wishing to be among the school's 70 scholars, 14 of whom are 'elected' each year, take an additional test. Non-scholars, known as Oppidans, are lodged in 25 houses scattered through the town; but each boy has his own room. There are a bewildering number of societies, including one named after George Orwell, which encourages dissidence, and Maynard Keynes, which inculcates the virtues of economics. Sports of all kinds are played with fervour, including such Eton-originated ones as the Wall Game, the Field Game (a bizarre hybrid featuring the least attractive aspects of soccer and rugby) and Eton Fives. In recent years, with the construction of a new, Olympic-quality rowing lake and featuring the patronage of Sir Matthew Pinsent (JWT 88, three Gold medals in the Sydney and Athens Olympics) rowing has taken pride of place.

Following a half-hearted, rapidly aborted experiment with sixth-formers and daughters of masters during the 1970s, the school has reverted to its historic, single-sex character – but with what is acknowledged to be a more generous system of leave that allows boys to get out more easily. Boys begin in F block, progressing through the school to A levels or to the international baccalaureate. Around 76 to 80 out of a year of roughly 260 boys end up at Oxford or Cambridge – a number that has remained consistent despite the rising standards of education at Eton, and the intense care taken to select only very bright pupils

Eton isn't quite the oldest school in Britain, but it remains the grandest. Founded on October 11th 1440 by a Royal Charter of Henry VI, it began as a religious institution destined for the care of 70 poor scholars and ten choristers. Such austerity, however, was compromised by the King's wish that the school should also furnish an education for the sons of the rich – and these lucky few, though there were later many more of them, were accommodated in bed-and-breakfast establishments situated within the town at a short distance from the cloister and chapel. From its beginnings, therefore, the school possessed a double function – that of providing a religious and secular elite (links were established from the beginning with King's College, Cambridge) and enabling social betters to keep up educationally with those who would serve them. Another feature of Eton retained through its history is self-government, which means something more than the ability to look after itself in consequence of an endowment. Eton's Provost is, by tradition and charter, appointed by the monarch; but its Vice-Provost and ten Fellows are chosen by a complicated system that puts the Vatican's procedures to shame: one being appointed by King's College, Cambridge (a sister endowment of Henry VI), one by the Senate of Cambridge, one by the Hebdomadal Council of Oxford, one by the Lord Chief Justice, one by the Head Master, the Lower Master and the Assistant Masters; and the remaining four by the Fellows themselves.

Eton's rulers have by and large been worldly and effective. They represent the same qualities – savoir faire, above all – for which their charges are famous. In miniature, they stand for the English way of doing things, through compromise and contacts in private, without extravagant declarations of principle. The current batch include a High Court judge, Sir Michael Burton (an Etonian, and specialist in commercial law, KS 64) and the head of Reading University Philosophy Department (Michael Proudfoot, specialist in the philosophy of the body, and the Masters' choice). There has never been a woman Head Master, House Master (though women, known picturesquely as Dames, used to run houses in the same capacity as House Masters do today – and the doyenne of them all, a Mrs. Evans, had an eponymous house, which still stands), or Provost; but there are currently two women Fellows, including the technocrat Baroness Hogg ex-governor of the BBC and chairman of the investment group 3i, and as this book went to press Dr Jane Grant was appointed Master-in-College.

These are merely the rawest, most basic Establishment-related facts associated with the 550-odd years of Eton's existence. It is a school, of course, where boys are sent to learn things, but a place, too, with many meanings. The experience of Eton, for good or bad, stretches through history. It owns many treasures deeded by Etonian well-wishers, including a Gutenberg Bible. And it is also a piece of British mythology, matching the royal family in the conviction it brings to the worship of a shared past. But this brings us to another important feature of Eton – the way in which, by virtue of what it is, the school is capable of arousing passions. Care about aspects of the British present, and you will not wish to remain neutral where Eton is concerned. For it remains a primary symbol of class and privilege in Britain. Even in a country so aggressively egalitarian as Britain – perhaps indeed, specially so – the fact of having gone to Eton remains a conversation-stopper, provoking silence or even an intake of breath. No other school, club or institution provokes a similar reaction. In some places it is these days dangerous, or at least disadvantageous, to speak of having been to Eton; and this, I reflect, is why the Head Master speaks jokingly of Eton being a 'four letter word,' and, not wholly misleadingly, of Etonians 'coming out' if they choose to they reveal their past.

***

I kill time in and around College yard, examining the buttress – all angles, making precision very difficult – from which College Fives was derived. Between the long stone-flagged paths are flints, cleaning of which used to be a punishment complementing the writing out, Homer Simpson-style, of dull Latin texts such as Virgil's *Georgics*. My favourite room is Upper School, used for school speeches and debates, and which was bombed in the Second World War. Busts of eighteenth-century worthies look over wooden benches and, at one end, there is a daïs of sorts for speakers. Eton has supplied eighteen Prime Ministers (nineteen if you count one from Northern Ireland) and here in

Between Chapel and School, 1937

this hall one can get a whiff of the arrogant, oligarchic, quasi-republican tradition of Eton. Adjoining it is the small room where, traditionally, floggings were administered, and below it the dark, primitive-looking Lower School, in which many centuries of carved names are preserved on primitive desks.

But I now approach the Provost's apartments down another corridor, via a line of black-and-white photographs commemorating recently famous Old Etonians such as the explorer-writer Wilfred Thesiger, Lords Longford, Carrington, Hurd and Home, and Harold Macmillan, first Earl of Stockton.

Sir Eric Anderson is tall, bushy-eyebrowed, with a slight limp and an outsize, super-burly presence. I realize that I am in awe of him. Formerly, he was Head Master at Eton, head of an Oxford College, and he was Tony Blair's house master at Fettes, known as 'the Scottish Eton'. (In 1997, Blair made use of Sir Eric in a promotional spot for the Teachers' Training Agency, with the slogan Nobody Forgets a Good Teacher.) Before that, he taught at Gordonstoun, the hale-and-hearty experimental institution where Prince Charles was educated. Sir Eric was an intimate of the Queen Mother (it was he who interviewed her; interviews to be used later-by whoever would become her "official" biographer after her death) and I recall from my notes that he is also a Knight of the Thistle, which is Scotland's highest honour, handpicked by the Queen.

An oar is fixed to the wall above the Provost's desk. From the eighteenth century onwards, leaving portraits were presented by eminent boys, and some of these hang on the walls, an informal guard of honour from the past. Interviewing Sir Eric is like receiving an audience, and I'm transported back in time. But he, too, is surprisingly frank when it comes to the expression of anxieties. He appears to regret the tendency of Eton to abandon its traditional base of pupils, taking pupils from the rest of the world or the many City rich, rather than country grandees or gents; though he also reiterates (an argument frequently voiced by those for whom tradition is important, in the Burkean sense, and change only acceptable if it can be fitted into the past) that the school has no choice.

'The fees are high, and they can't be kept down,' he tells me. 'Eton is subject to the same regulations regarding wheelchair access, or the requirement for adults to be on duty on the school premises 24 hours a day as any lesser educational establishment.' The Provost raises awesome eyebrows, speaking confidently and with the periodic hesitations that appear to come naturally to the British educational elite. 'The time may come when few native English can afford to send their sons to Eton,' he says. 'And if that happens, the school will have lost any pretence to be training a cross-section of Britain's. We pause, confronted by the gravity of such sentiments. 'It would be a sad state of affairs, and we're doing everything to avoid it,' he says.

I am intrigued by the notion that Eton did ever represent a cross-section of anything except the elite which it both created and then came to represent. I ask whether the training of an elite was ever practised consciously at Eton. Maybe it just happened that way – and perhaps the connection could cease to exist, just as naturally. There's no divinely instituted relationship between Eton, power and achievement, I suggest. But I am not sure whether the Provost gets my drift – indeed why should he?

He laughs, listing new and successful types of Old Etonians: entrepreneurs, actors, media people. 'People are still prepared to make sacrifices in order to send their children to Eton,' he assures me. From Paul Dacre, editor of the *Daily Mail*, through Bill Wyman of the Rolling Stones and Aleksandr Solzhenitsyn, taking in any number of nouveaux (or indeed not quite so nouveaux) riches, they continue to request entry on behalf of gifted sons. Eton, the Provost implies, is a testimony to the flexibility of the English (from the lips of this Scotsman, the word Britain never occurs in connection with the school). He outlines a new scheme to raise Old Etonian money, doubling the endowment of the school within the next ten years. This will enable the school either to freeze its fees or increase the number of scholarships. Many more bright boys seeking admission could then be accommodated. 'In the future there will be nothing unusual about being paid for if you are an Etonian,' he assures me. 'That's how it is with good universities in the United States, and that's how we would like it to be here.'

This evocation of a merit-based, snobbery-free Eton utopia stops me dead in my tracks. I tell the Provost about a recent visit to Eton. While watching the Wall Game, and raking notes, I had been accosted by a man who turned out to be a bodyguard. He wanted to know why I was there. Was I really an Etonian, and, if so, why was I taking notes? Was I in the employment of a tabloid? It took me a while to realise that I had unconsciously transgressed on to a patch of mud made significant by the royal presence of Prince Harry playing the Wall Game. I want to ask the Provost who fits into the contemporary scheme of Eton, and how. It caters most of all these days for the rich who are also very bright. Is it also, as it was supposed to be, a place for the not so rich and very bright? Are boys in the latter category drawn from the middle classes, as in the past, or do the poor actually get a proper look in? Do the merely averagely talented cope (in the past a large proportion of Etonians) – or not at all?

These are not questions easily posed at Eton, and I am not surprised that the Provost prefers to talk about other things. He sits at the centre of a network of high-placed informers. Like most Foreign Office mandarins – still drawn from the ranks of Etonians, even if recruitment to the less glamorous domestic Civil Service has fallen off – he expresses disapproval of the Iraq war. (It comes as a surprise to find this grand Tory so plainly, unequivocally antagonistic towards George Bush's America – and this increases my respect for him.) He nods favourably in the direction of his former pupil Tony Blair, while expressing conventional worries about the prospect of a Britain supervised by an egalitarian Scot such as Gordon Brown. Michael Howard, a son of whom did well at the school, he commends, 'a nice man despite his reputation'. As he rises, dismissing me cheerfully in the style of those with a near-lifetime of uncontested authority, he says: 'People think of Eton as not changing easily. We have a history of modernising in the English way, without appearing to do so very dramatically. And we do change, more often than many other institutions.'

***

Before returning to London, I linger again around the yard. Pieces of half-remembered architectural detail – mottling on the side of the chapel, the dense redness of brick, the clock on the tower with a bluish sky behind it – detach themselves from the past. These are simple things, accidentally assembled, but one can reconfigure them endlessly, making new patterns, as I suppose I have done in my life. This is how personal memories are transformed. This is how having 'been' somewhere can acquire a greater collective significance. And this is how one comes conclusively to belong. Perhaps this is even how one learns to think of oneself (the impersonal third person is *de rigueur* here) as being English, belonging to England, being someone.

The cloister just below the Provost's quarters is lined with simple stone tablets commemorating Eton sons fallen in battle. I can stand before these stones, and be made swiftly and heart-breakingly aware of the place in Britain of Eton life. During the four-odd years of what is still called the Great War, an entire year of Etonians died, mostly, as the inscriptions attest, in the Flanders mud; and another year were wounded – figures which bring their death rate to the levels endured by Highland regiments, or by the hapless imperial contingents drafted from India for death near Ypres. Old Etonians won 13 V.C.s, 548 D.S.O.s and a heart-stopping 744 Military Crosses. There were no less than 31 Old Etonian generals, some of them more competent than others, among them the steely technocrat Sir Henry Rawlinson (later Lord), second-in-command during the 1916 Somme slaughter, who encompassed the final destruction of the German armies in 1918, and who was later sent as the commander of the allied force which attempted, without much success, to overthrow the Bolshevik regime.

In the midst of so many Eton names, here is Julian Grenfell, who wrote the marvellous poem *Into Battle* shortly before he was hit in the head by shrapnel, dying in great pain in a field hospital in northern France:

> The thundering line of battle stands,
> And in the air Death moans and sings;
> But Day shall clasp with strong hands
> And Night shall fold him in soft wings.

Grenfell was a tough, handsome, wholly exceptional young man, a puritan who wrote polemics directed against the laziness of his own class, and who, even as a boy, saw much to criticise in the feckless aspects of Eton life, but an aesthete, too. Grenfell's poems were printed in the *Times,* and it is far from fanciful to think of him becoming a great national bard, ranked with Kipling, but less cruelly obsessed with certainties.

I think of the Provost, and his hopeful list of new-style Old Etonians fitted to succeed in the new century. It's good to know that Eton is capable of producing actors like Hugh Laurie, and entrepreneurs, too, like Johnnie Boden. But I am here for another reason, too. I am interested to know whether, stretching through history, slouching and drawling, there is a recognisable Eton type. Certainly, beginning with the over-quoted line about the battle of Waterloo, mistakenly attributed to the Duke of Wellington, the world assumes this to be the case. Etonians merely shrug when the subject is mentioned. The matter of being Eton is too obvious, or too endlessly complicated, or both. And yet these stones tell a different story. It's interesting to see that so many grieving parents sought to preserve the memory of their boys within the context of the school they had just attended. One can't explain this fact only with the thought that, tragically, this was where they had last been seen free and happy, in possession of their future. I recall that the Head Master's nice, worried wife half-jokingly chided me for wanting to write still more about Eton, and that I fumbled my answer. I might have said that I want to find out what it is that stays in the air across the centuries, granting the stones around me so much influence. I should have said simply that I want to know what it means to be Eton.

People tell me, of course, that the school has changed. Life is softer, without beating, and, like the rest of Britain,

Eton appears less aberrant. Indeed blandness is said to be characteristic of the boys. In particular, I am told by current Etonians, no-one cares about politics much. The debates are poorly attended, and when one was planned on the future of the monarchy, and the authorities expressed due reservations, fearing negative publicity, it was cancelled. However, ten Etonians did attend the march against the Iraq war. (They were allowed to, whereas a larger group were forbidden to demonstrate on behalf of hunting.) One master bemoans the 'default Tory position' of boys. 'Adolescents are conservative,' he says, somewhat lamely.

A boy I get to know tells me how the old school cult of 'effortless ease' now merely means that one works with no special imaginative input. But I am by now used to the relatively glum notion that, in Britain at least, everything goes from bad to worse. I don't believe this has happened to Eton. Certainly, the school is less aggressively bizarre, or so it would appear. The dullards have gone, which may or may not be a pity. I cannot become indignant about the loss of coal fires, or beds that fold down from the wall, or indeed the greater freedom given to boys when it comes to going home for the weekend. But the basis of the school appears unchanged. It is still single-sexed, obsessed with its own rules, status-crazy. For all I know, aspects of its strange sexual mores may linger on. I cannot see why its snobberies should be extinguished. And I do anyhow recall what the same master calls 'the fat-bottomed Tory' element of Eton. Isn't that what the school was supposed, in part at least, to produce?

I am given pause by another visit, this time to Michael Meredith, who is known as the College Librarian, but who for the past 40 years (after a brief time teaching America) has acted as memory to the school, and, it would seem, as conscience. I remember being taught by him and I am surprised to hear others criticise his disciplinarian's approach to literature. Meredith is small, impeccably dressed, precise in expression, with neat, darting hands and eyes that appear to be shy behind their steel-rimmed lenses.

It is clear that he is devoted, not just to Eton and literature, but to rare books. Another, less expected side of him emerges as he shows me such treasures as an eighteenth-century map of St. Petersburg, of which only three are in existence. Meredith loves all forms of old-fashioned excellence, and he has fought on their behalf, and against the conservatism of the school. He believes that these things should be available to anyone capable of valuing them. This is why he opened this magnificent, panelled suite of rooms to the public. But it is also why, as a House Master, he appears to have solicited scholarship boys personally, securing their admission and, if it proved necessary, going outside

Eton itself in search of money for them.

Fingering rare books, he tells me about X, the 'grounds-man's son', or Y, who was a Pakistani from Slough, 'son of a shopkeeper'. 'They fitted in,' he says, with conviction, though I wonder how they did.

In Meredith's care the school has begun to accumulate the works of non-Etonians. Browning and Hardy figure here as a consequence of his efforts, and I sense that this is an apology for the school's self-absorption. We go to a newly refurbished part of the library in which an astounding collection of First World War books are kept, including first editions of Sassoon and Owen. I find that I want to ask Meredith where so much of Eton has got him, and whether the place fulfilled his dreams. However, two members of the history department arrive in order to view the new installation, and the moment passes.

'I didn't really talk enough about Eton,' he says, waving me into the dusk. But it occurs to me that he did, as much as I could expect. 'Don't, whatever you do, use the word toff,' he shouts in my direction. 'It's so vulgar, and it's so appallingly misleading.'

On another visit, I meet the editors of the school magazine, the *Eton Chronicle*, and get to address members of the Orwell Society at Eton. The topic is 'Why Work in the Media?'; and the audience, as a consequence of the

American elections, as I am politely told at dinner, will be small. Of course, I do not mind. I do my best to say that the old stable configuration of careers has been smashed. In the media they will either cleverly make money as entrepreneurs or (not a wholly attractive prospect for Etonians) be made to suffer like the society's founder, for wishing to tell the truth about things. I suggest that the establishment media have died anyhow, and that they might as well be bold. There aren't many boys, but their questions are astounding. How do they know so much at this tender age? Knowing too much, having too much at an early age comes with its own catastrophes; so it has been with many I know. Eton can be dangerous for you. But I resolve to put the neat shapes of hindsight behind me for the moment as I walk out with my escorts into the blackness of School Yard. This is, above all, a beautiful place, and one that thinks of itself as being good. Eton says that one must be rich, and successful, and still be good. Being Eton, one must be all these things.

CHAPTER THREE

So let us start where it matters most, with the greatest Eton mystery of all. How is it that a school for boys of only moderately larger than average size has acquired so much influence, being regarded as a place capable of defining an entire civilisation? There must be some black magic at work here, and indeed there is. Eton surrounds itself with its own mythology, but Eton myths are helped into existence by the reactions of outsiders.

'*Quel supplice,*' the French mandarin homosexual writer , André Gide, is said to have remarked on catching sight of so many youths attired in black. '*Cela me coupe l'appétit,*' he added after seeing Collegers wolf down their food.

'How sublime in conception, how grotesque in execution,' the American literary critic, Lionel Trilling, mumured in contemplation of damaged specimens of school dress.

The playwright Alan Bennett, wrote a script about the Old Etonian drunk, promiscuous homosexual and KGB spy, Guy Burgess, and the film featured a horrified Thora Hird examining the contents of Burgess's wardrobe in Moscow, with its soup-stained O.E. ties, and its wrecked bespoke suits from the High Street tailor Tom Brown. 'You pissed in our soup,' she says, succinctly, of his betrayal of England. I am interested to learn that Bennett still retains an impression, gathered at Cambridge, that Etonians are 'exotic creatures'. (The irony highlights Bennett's own, end-lessly played out self-deprecation, but it implies, too, that Etonians may not be quite as splendid as they make them-selves out to be.)

Perhaps the bizarreness of Eton is more evident if you don't know it from the inside. In what must have been a scene worthy of an early Evelyn Waugh novel, the construc-tivist photographer Moholy-Nagy, who had emigrated to Britain and was short of money, was hired to illustrate a posh art book. Crouching, spying from odd angles, he ren-dered 1930s Eton as a series of blank vistas, or geometrical patterns in which specimens of the upper class were to be observed either purposelessly marching up and down, com-pulsively eating, or languidly going about their business. One can see Etonians here as a strange tribe, uncomfortable in their strange garb, near autistic in their obliviousness to others. A close-up of bananas and ice cream entitled 'Eton Caviar' alone hints at some sort of submerged hedonism among the ill-smelling socks, scuffed shoes, and incomprehensible sporting tallies.

The Eton mystique appears greatest from a distance, as the Foreign Secretary Anthony Eden discovered when he went to talk to Adolf Hitler in Berchtesgaden in the months before Munich. Thinking that geographical proximity on the Western Front might create some ground for small talk, he had hoped to exchange war memories with the Führer. But the Führer was convinced that Britain owed its victory in the Great War over Germany to the military ethos of Eton. How otherwise could one explain the defeat of Prussian discipline? We are here confronted with a lost episode of *Blackadder*, or a vintage piece of Wodehouse. Over the chintzes, the *kaffee* and the Wagnerian view, Eden attempted to set the Führer right. The Eton College Corps was a shambles, under-equipped. (The uniform 'wasn't khaki, it was a sort of milk chocolate/wine colour, with pale blue facing', a contemporary observer recalls. 'You took what you could get out of the pool that more or less fitted you, and it didn't fit very well...') Soldiering wasn't compulsory, although the boys who joined up endured the marches and counter-marches with good humour. But all the Führer wanted to talk about was Eton mastery.

There are other truths or half-truths that originate nearer home, with Etonians themselves. A first, founding myth of Eton consists in the assumption that merely being at the school conveys a special importance. 'Well, it was the only place,' declared Lord Longford, Labour peer, Cabinet Minister, don, and, in his old age penal reformer and grand eccentric. 'I didn't really take anywhere else very seriously. And for Etonians there is no other school, I mean it's like the Catholic Church in its triumphalist moments.'

Nicholas Coleridge, editorial director of Condé Nast, describes this widely held feeling quite simply, in a more modern idiom. 'If I meet somebody that I have never met before… and it emerges that they were there, I feel an interest in them that is multiplied by ten,' he says. Coleridge also admits to asking himself about certain acquaintances who weren't at Eton: 'Now, why weren't they?… I do accept that I prefer the company of Etonians to the company of people from other public schools.' He tells the story of being stuck in a taxi somewhere in the Moroccan desert and playing a game with a fellow-Etonian. They had an hour to write down on a piece of paper the names of all the Eton contemporaries they could remember. If a name was written down by both of them, they got one point, and if only one of them got the name he scored two points. Then there were 'people that you can hardly remember were there at all but suddenly, when their name is mentioned, they come back to you with a terrible clarity.' Three points were awarded for reclaiming these near-unknown Etonians from oblivion. Coleridge and his friend must have assumed that, in any identical game played by fellow-Etonians, they themselves wouldn't have been three-pointers.

A barely secondary myth, feeding off the notion of Eton's importance, is the deeply rooted idea that the school breeds a unique relationship with individual liberty. This is most clearly delineated in one of the most eloquent recently published school memoirs, *Wars and Shadows,* by General Sir David Fraser. Here it is asserted confidently that 'Eton believed in liberty, in the old, brutal sense of leaving people to get on in their own way.' The General – who served in the Grenadier Guards in the Second World War, coming to adulthood in the ruins of Germany, and later supervising the withdrawal from Empire – depicts Eton as an eighteenth-century Whig utopia miraculously preserved in the 1930s. Instead of would-be dictators, his noble Eton is filled with school Hampdens:

Eton was more like the world than any other school: it had more tolerance, perhaps suffered more evil, perhaps enabled more good. I have said that it was built on the belief in liberty. It was also something of a relic of an aristocratic or pre-Victorian past. It did not seek to turn out 'gentlemen'. In fact I don't think it seeks, or in my day sought, to turn out any particular article. We were not greatly pressed upon or stifled by the team spirit, the need to conform.

In his understated Eton way, Sir David reminds us that Eton wasn't like other public schools. It didn't require pupils to wear military uniforms each day. 'Particular articles' – the word is redolent of snobbery in relation to 'trade' – were not manufactured here. And Eton didn't have to strive to inculcate any superiority, even an effortless one – because it had no need to do so. In this way, in the eyes of Etonians and non-Etonians alike, the school snobbery could be made useless, seeming gratuitous and thus more palatable. But Fraser also insists, convincingly, on the modernity of Eton, which is evident in the willingness of Etonians like himself to fight for civilisation. So Eton, like it or not, was indeed a superior place.

For others Eton is both more exotic, and less unequivocally part of the natural order of things. It remains what French historians saw in Victorian England – a place in which many forms of society, elsewhere extinct, are to be found miraculously preserved, and in good nick. This is how Cyril Connolly, ex-Colleger, history scholarship winner, essayist and novelist looks back untranquilly at school:

> In practice Eton was not a democracy for the system was feudal. The masters represented the church, with the headmaster as Pope; the boys, with their hierarchy of colours and distinctions, were the rest of the population, while the prefects and athletes, the captains of houses and the members of Pop were the feudal overlords who punished offences at the request of the 'church' and in return were tacitly allowed to break the same rules themselves...

Many Etonians agree that the Eton experience is fundamental and irreversible, more important than attending university (plainly an anticlimax), getting married (no big deal after all those crushes, and best done chummily with the sister of a friend), falling ill or dying. The purpose of being an Etonian, according to this traditional view, is to secure a job in which one can mingle with other O.E.s, squabble, conspire, or divide the spoils when appropriate, join the clubs they attend, assure that one's male heirs go to Eton, and that any daughters marry Etonians. Anything else in life is no more than an afterthought.

***

I don't know why, but I tend to think of Etonians as rude guests at a party. They stand together in a circle, talking about things which are of exclusive concern to them. When you approach, the circle parts easily; but they stop talking. With respect to the rest of the world they adopt a posture of polite exclusion. I've lost track of the number of times I have heard arrogance ascribed to Etonians, and, just as inevitably, the sense of ease, or security. Ask how these qualities are to be identified, and one's interlocutor becomes vague, as if to say that it's obvious, why bother to ask. One City acquaintance describes a tendency of Etonians to imagine that they make the rules, and he cites as an example a particular and obvious instance of insider trading. The Etonian, he remarks with surprising bitterness, was unable to see what was wrong. For what reason, other than legitimated gain, does an Etonian enter business? 'He didn't see it,' my friend suggests. 'And you might say that this was because his whole life was based on some sort of cheating – the notion that he was in some way special.'

Much has been written, in this context, about the celebrated Claremont gambling club, most of whose members came from Eton, and who appeared, like the feckless and stupid Lord Lucan, to believe that they were above the law, and therefore permitted to do things like murdering a wife, or clubbing a nanny to death. In support of this notion the career of Sir James Goldsmith, member of that notorious gambling club, financial speculator and sometime raffish politician, is adduced. Young Jimmy detested both Eton and his House Master to such a degree that he bought the latter a set of records as a leaving present and, having proffered them, took them out of their sleeves and broke them one by one, throwing the pieces across the study.

Eton breeds gentlemen, and to the rest of the world it appears that a gentleman must never bestir himself excessively. From this, and from the appearance of impracticability, comes the notion that Etonians needn't do very much. The school itself appears to be divided on this question, uncertain whether it is indeed a breeding ground for drones, or something much tougher. As far back as the 1850s one can find those who say that it just isn't fair how well the least-equipped Etonians do:

I should have a different story to tell of those who were addicted to drinking, bad language, stealing, idleness, etc. and what do I find?... Why of course I should have to point to mental and physical wrecks, men who have dragged hitherto a miserable existence... Now what do I find? That those very boys have become Cabinet

Ministers, statesmen. Officers, clergymen, country gentlemen etc.

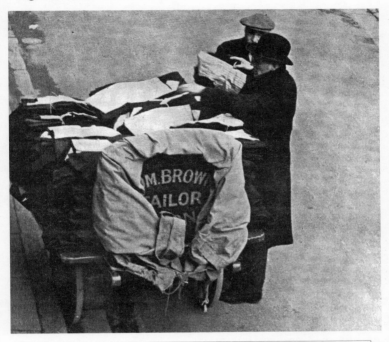

The tailor's barrow bringing around the clothes, cleaned and pressed, for Sunday and the week to come, 1937

Are Etonians really undeserving and idle? Not so, comes the riposte. In some mysterious way, the fact of having been at Eton has educated them. This is the meaning of an Eton education as described by a nineteenth-century teacher William Johnson:

But you go to a great school not so much for knowledge as for arts and habits: for the habit of attention, for the act of assuming at a moment's notice a new intellectual position, for the art of entering quickly into another person's thoughts, for the habit of submitting to censure and refutation, for the art of indicating assent and dissent in graduated terms, for the habit of regarding minute points of accuracy...

It's alright to have done, or learnt nothing, at school. One can merely have studied *how to be.*

Another acquaintance in the City (not an Etonian) describes the peculiar style of work of Etonians. 'They don't easily adapt to large groups and they have, bizarrely, no external concept of hierarchy,' he explains. 'If you leave them to their devices, however, they will organise themselves into syndicates, in the eighteenth-century style, and end by making lots of money.'

Etonians, it is alleged, have problems with such banal conventions as the traffic code. In the old days they disregarded licensing laws. Among Etonians (the accusation has been levelled at myself) the existence of a servant class is taken for granted. I have an Etonian friend whose routine even when young and unfogeyish was invariably, when arriving in any bar or hotel, to ask for something not available. 'God,' he moaned, as the hapless waiter went in search of it, as if to say that nothing could be relied on. If the commodity or service was produced, he felt satisfied by having insisted on maintaining standards; if it wasn't, he experienced a mild sense of thwarted superiority. Perhaps so much *savoir faire* does imply ownership of a kind.

'Etonians are good to be around,' the psychologist Oliver James (also an Etonian) says. 'They have a fundamentally optimistic view of life. Temperamentally, they're Bertie Woosters. If the sun shines on you for so much of your early life, you tend to think it has been put there for that express purpose.'

But of course Etonians do still own things, as they always have done. I recall a train journey through England in the company of a Viscount who identified pieces of wasteland by the track with the information that this family or that one had once owned pieces of it. 'We have been able to last,' William told me. 'And at least we didn't get our heads cut off. I suppose Eton did have something to do with that – after all, it's a place to which aristocrats went in order to meet people who were both less rich than them, and perhaps more intelligent. They might not marry your sister, but you should know them. They could always help with raising loans on the value of land.' Suddenly I became aware of exactly why such apparently recondite subjects as land enclosure or the relation between aristocracy, gentry and the crown in the 1640s received so much attention in Eton history classes – because it is necessary to know certain things about a world of which you are an owner in title.

The Right Rev. Simon Barrington-Ward, an OE, recalled paying homage to the Queen when be became a bishop, and how a schoolfriend of his stood by her side, holding the oath he was to read. 'It's almost dream-like,' he observed about so many Etonians sharing membership of the Establishment. 'There is an incongruous sense that we are all play-acting and that we will go back and find that we are just starting again. I do have that strange feeling of: Will we wake up and find that we are still there?'

The Eton worldliness comes tinged with this strange untouchability. Can one be so worldly and, at the same time, remain removed from things by so much entitlement? I can recall being intrigued when an Eton-obsessed film director friend depicted life after Eton as an extension of the Grand Tour. We were sitting at the Cannes Film Festival, surrounded by movie world hustlers, when he began to enumerate what in his eyes were the great Etonian limitations. 'For Etonians, the world exists primarily as an object of patronage, never wholly to be viewed on equal terms, in a spirit of total engagement, and the detachment of Etonians is ultimately crippling,' he explained to me over cups of espresso. 'Etonians are consumers and patrons, not creators – they think they know so much, even if they don't,' he explained. 'And they go from one enthusiasm to another inconstantly, but always with the same flirtatious dogmatism. Perhaps they are the ultimate amateurs, just as they represent in extreme form the old gentleman culture.'

I get something of the same criticism when I drive out to a nondescript building on the edge of London. This is the headquarters of the mail order and retail business Boden. Its chairman, Johnnie Boden works out of a smallish office adjoining racks of samples. Boden is 40-ish, fresh-faced, energetic, good-looking in a Victorian cricketer way (I learn that he was indeed in the Eton XI, and a member of Pop) and he is very proud of the business he has created. Although he says he loved Eton, he did find it difficult. It is he who draws attention to the oddest paradox of the school – that while claiming to develop individuality, it nonetheless sustains its own style of conformism. At a loss, Boden went into the City after 'uni'. ('All Etonians seem to go there. It's so easy for them.') He thought briefly of returning to Eton, in order to teach, before stumbling into the business he now runs.

'Etonians like to say they make great entrepreneurs, but they are in fact terrible,' he says. 'A lot of business is boring, and they don't like that. They'd rather do cool things.

Working really hard isn't cool. And then there's the insufferable Eton side – the pompousness, the need to belong to an establishment. So they do safe things – like law or media. To succeed – really, really succeed as a businessman – you have to be prepared to make a fool of yourself. I just don't see that as a very Etonian thing.' But Boden now appears worried that he might seem too negative, and he backtracks, telling me how many good Etonian friends he has, and how often he sees them. 'Etonians are never chippy,' he says. 'It's so bad to be chippy, such a waste of life.' He looks at me with strong brown eyes, communicating wisdom. 'Never be chippy,' he says.

Notoriously, British culture is constructed around notions of personal style. With its clothes, its slouch, its odd fashions combining with irremovable traditions, Eton is frequently depicted as if it were the originator of British toff style. The fashion of Mockney (speaking as if one were doomed to the flattened vowels of Estuary English) has long been prevalent in Eton. Chav attire (loud Burberry pattern hats, garish shorts etc.) was worn by Etonians as an act of conspicuous vulgarity long before the word was invented. The Rolling Stones were for many years the Eton rock band of choice. Meanwhile, Etonians are celebrated for their brass, their ability to say in tight spots that something will not do. James Bond is a (somewhat déclassé) Etonian who got kicked out of Eton for having an affair with a boys' maid. (Ian Fleming wasn't kicked out himself, but he appears not to have liked Eton. He was, however, a successful runner, and when the author Paul Gallico alluded to Fleming winning a race just after a birching, with his shorts bloodied, as the reason for both his fascination with sadism and an 'implacable hatred' of Eton, Fleming crossed the passage out. 'I had a mysterious affection for the place,' he wrote. 'So much for sadism.')

One of my favourite expressions of the Eton *sang froid* style comes from American writer, Fleur Cowles's description of the otherwise mild travel writer, Robert Byron, confronted by a roomful of Nazis after a Nuremberg rally:

I saw a red flush rising on Robert's neck and the next moment I heard him saying in a deadly voice: 'What happens on the continent is always England's concern. Every now and then we are unfortunate enough to be led by a Chamberlain – but that's only temporary. Don't be misguided. In the end we always rise up and smash the tyrannies that threaten Europe. We have smashed them before, and I warn you we will smash them again.'

This is how we all want Etonians to behave, after all – as

heroes with a touch of old-fashioned class. But there is something, too, in the notion that Etonians, being habituated to the proximity of power, make their peace with the status quo over-easily.

'When the facts change, I change my mind,' the economist Maynard Keynes (a Colleger, certainly a genius, perhaps the greatest Englishman of his time after Churchill, and a promiscuous homosexual – at least until his marriage in middle age to a Russian ballerina – whose sexual career is thought to have begun at Eton) remarked testily, when taxed with inconsistency. During the First World War, Keynes was able to work at the Treasury, receiving much praise for furthering a war that he had come (not even privately) to abhor. When his pacifist Bloomsbury friends were outraged, David Garnett came up with a simple explanation. Keynes was motivated by the system of rewards he had first experienced at Eton:

It all comes back to what you and Ottoline (Morrell) were talking about after dinner. Whether one minds being caned at school. You, guided by your intellect, have set yourself in a position where you won't be caned. I, guided by my body, have aroused in me a degree of hate that comes to nothing more practical than intestinal derangement.

Keynes was a super-patriot as well as a genius. Despite his famous remark ('In the long run, we are all dead,' he once told a verbose civil servant) he believed that it was best to hang on, waiting for better times. But Garnett was right – Keynes wasn't a resigner, and sometimes this seems like opportunism. It is possible to admire everything about Keynes' life – his heroic perseverance in the face of illness as much as his stubbornness in rescuing causes in which he believed – while wondering how he would have survived if removed from the comforts of power. Many Etonian mandarins appear to share this trait. Loving power, they do change their minds, but without realising it – or without bothering to ascertain whether the facts have indeed changed. In bureaucracies this allows speedy promotion, suaveness greasing the wheels of advancement. Mrs. Thatcher made a famous crack about her cabinet containing as many Old Estonians as Old Etonians, but observers also tell us how much she enjoyed having Etonians around to boss. Most of them were fired when they were no longer useful, but there is no record of any coherent revolt against her will.

***

Is Eton really so special? Are Etonians really so different? The Eton mystique often seems a matter of mirrors, a collusion between those hungry for notoriety and Etonians who are only to happy to supply it. But I am speedily put right on this matter by the novelist John Le Carré, who taught at Eton as a young man under his real name Cornwell, and for whom, as he explains in impassioned detail, the school was 'a secondary education in privilege.' Cornwell directs me to *A Murder Of Quality*, an early novel featuring a school called Carne and a cast of snobbish, sexually repressed beaks – and a killer whose motive is the concealment of homosexual acts committed many years ago. 'I meant it to be like Eton,' he explains. 'At that moment a certain amount of camouflage seemed necessary.' Certainly, the camouflage is successful, because the school depicted seems both less grand and more philistine. But this early work does show just how intensely the author loathes the system of private education in Britain.

And yet it seems, as we talk, that Cornwell's views about Eton are distinctly more complicated, arising from a passionate ambivalence that the years have entirely failed to chill. He remembers being told by an older master during his first week at Eton that he mustn't wear a gown when riding a bicycle. What he characterises as the 'cool impertinence' of those he taught remains with him. 'The boys were adult, funny, a little removed from life even as they evolved effortlessly into the shrewdest operators. They were at once innocent and worldly.' Discerning in their speech, they communicated with each other in codes that still fascinate him. 'Most of all, I felt, they really knew how to be with each other, and that was the real Eton thing, that was what you learnt.'

Cornwell recalls a meeting many years later, when he worked at the Foreign Office, and the prospects of one Etonian were debated. Should so-and-so be sent to a crucial posting in Cold War Berlin? 'Offstage, someone remarked in a casual fashion that he just wouldn't do, and the rest of the room coalesced immediately around this position. Why, the man drove an Alvis, he employed an exotic servant from his previous posting in the Sudan, God knows where, his wife made too bold an impression – the truth was that he was wrong. And that was that. I assume that was the end of his career – but the really remarkable thing was how quickly it could be done, and with how little fuss.' I ask Cornwell whether he admires such expressions of group solidarity. 'Yes, I suppose I do,' he says. Then I ask him whether he can truly recognise Etonians across a crowded room, and he laughs. 'I'm right 80 per cent of the time,' he says, in his strong schoolmaster's or actor's voice. 'Over the years I've learned to anticipate failure. You say: "You weren't by any chance at school with X?" Or: "Weren't you in Y's house? Really not. Oh I am sorry, I would have thought so." And of course, the English are such snobs that they're flattered even if they weren't at the place at all.' Le Carré's work is filled with brilliant moments taken from the British social system in which people only talk to those with whom they share things, excluding others – novel after novel displays the institutional autism of elite Britain. And, perhaps, navigation in a closed milieu is a significant Eton skill.

Nonetheless there is a rationale behind such persistent rituals, as Cornwell observes. He believes that Etonians did embody, from the eighteenth century through to Mrs. Thatcher, some aspect of service to country. Eton existed to foster the links between class, talent and nation. He wonders whether the tradition isn't extinct. Its loss, or perhaps the question of whether it had ever existed, is a principal theme of his novels, filled as they are with Etonians sometimes half-trying and often not quite succeeding to do the right thing. (Good Etonians alternate with bad Etonians throughout the Le Carré oeuvre. The bad are bought for a high price without admitting that they have sold themselves; the good, the real English stuff, by contrast, like Justin Quayle, hero of *The Constant Gardener,* come shabbily dressed, despised for their gentleness and beloved of wild, usually foreign women.) 'Eton has never wholly let go of me,' Cornwell concedes. Recently, in an interview given to the *Times,* he said that Prime Minister Anthony Eden had visited Eton in search of spiritual guidance even as he dragged Britain into war over the Suez canal in 1956. He suggested that Eden was a bit fey. What degree of insecurity, perhaps sexual, lay behind Eden's dandyish wardrobes? Was it true that he wore double-breasted pyjamas?

Cornwell remembered drafting a letter signed by ten junior masters, in which opposition to the Suez War was vigorously opposed. But he was shocked to discover that perhaps his memory had betrayed him. 'The letter was never published in the *Times* – well, perhaps it was intercepted by one of the school bigwigs,' Cornwell says. 'Lady Avon let me know that her late husband had never sought solace during the Suez crisis. Indeed, according to his biographer, he never enjoyed being at Eton, showing no attachment to its rituals, though I have to stress that he did, like any good O.E., send both sons there.' Cornwell giggles, affecting shock at such revelations. 'I was mortified,' he explains. 'But you know, perhaps these things weren't true – either one's memory does betray the facts, or, just as likely, one can simply have been under the Eton spell.'

***

Among so many questions of precedence, personal style etc, a cruder question remains. Are Etonians snobbish? The

1960s novel *The Fourth of June*, by the Etonian David Benedictus, depicts snobbery as a disease which everyone connected with Eton – beaks, horrible mothers, disgustingly cruel prefects, only the odd scholarship boy remaining immune – is bound to suffer. The Etonian editor of the *Tatler*, who is dashing, fluent, and called Geordie Greig, insists to me that, reputation notwithstanding, Etonians are not snobbish. 'It's a media invention,' he says confidently. 'When I worked at the *South East London Mercury*, people didn't care that I was an Etonian. Perhaps Etonians can afford not to be snobbish. I've always found other public schools far more snobbish than Eton. Don't you acknowledge the existence of the "wannabe factor"?'

I think about Eton and snobbery. There's an Eton friend whom I will call, unoriginally, X. He came from a somewhat posher, more squireish family than myself, married well and now enjoys a well-heeled life in New York. I like him very much and see him occasionally. Others I know, however, dislike aspects of him, even while they freely acknowledge his overwhelming charm. They say he's a snob and, when I take his side, they retort that, being an Etonian myself, I am blind. Eton has made me unable to see how snobbish he really is. 'He talks to you in a certain way, with so much charm,' they say. 'You just don't see how he talks to other people. And you don't notice how he uses contacts.' Snobs are social climbers; as Thackeray pointed out, snobbery can be read as an instance, however misguided, of self-improvement. But one can surely have everything, and be a snob. These are the real Eton snobs.

Of all Eton qualities, tribalism is, understandably, the most enduring one, passing through the centuries. A primary ritual familiar to the tribe is the obituary. Once upon a time, Etonian obituaries appeared in the *Times,* but they have more recently also graced the pages of the *Daily Telegraph.* Almost invariably, a photograph shows the subject as he once was, young and dashing, his time spent at Eton occupies pride of place:

At Eton in the 1950s the name Marsden was synonymous with rowing – and with winning. John Marsden's grandfather had made rowing history as a Cambridge man who had been lured to Oxford, where he stroked the university to victory in the boat race of 1864... John's father had reached the Ladies' Plate at Henley, and John himself, as Eton Master, set out with single-minded determination, to match their efforts. Every day, after teaching, John would drive to Putney, to train for the Wingfield Sculls, the amateur championship of England. He rowed 3,000 practice miles before he reckoned he was ready. After five attempts, at the age of 41, he won. (The *Times*, April 8th 2004)

I can recall Marsden only as a man who taught German very badly, rubbing his testicles in class. Others, however, will read such tributes in a spirit of generalised nostalgia.

Improbably, ravages of time notwithstanding, the Eton world does endure. Like the idylls of silliness depicted in PG Wodehouse, this never-lost Eton is something to go back to in whatever bizarre place or moment of your life you find yourself. This theme is given rich expression in the countless memoirs of Etonians-in-Empire, but a more recent version can be found in an account of an Old Etonian Subcontinent Dinner, published in the school's annual *Old Boys'* magazine in 2004:

The formal dinner, by kind permission of H.E. Mark Lyall-Grant and his wife Sheila, seating 24, was held at the British High Commissioner's Residence and garden complete with a statue of Queen Victoria – Mark coming from a long line of Indian administrators. We enjoyed a superb dinner and excellent wine. The young son of a Pakistani diplomat provided piano support for the Boating Song and School Song. The author's speech (a Waugh-named Roddy Sole) included the speech from Lord Curzon's speech… 'The East is a University whether the scholar never takes his degree (sic).'

The best memories outlive the worst ones. When the Fascist leader Oswald Mosley was locked up in Wormwood Scrubs in 1940, his son Nicholas was gratified to discover that at Eton no-one mentioned this fact – not because it was deemed unimportant but because his presence alone at the school was considered evidence of his worth. Mosley *fils* recalled this episode with pleasure more than 50 years later. When I asked him how someone as left-wing as he had become could still be touched by Eton, he paused before replying. 'One does, you know,' he replied. 'It's funny but one never gets over it.'

Can anyone not educated at Eton enter this closed world? No wonder that it is thought that Etonians, having learnt to be with each other, help each other out in life. The fantasy of a Masonic network of school tie worthies consorting with each other in a determined effort to retain the best jobs is surprisingly durable. My own hunch is that there may be something in this notion, but the reality is probably less sensational. Etonians needn't choose between conflicting loyalties. They are brought up with the assumption that one can have it every way. Eton loyalty complements other forms of loyalty – to country, class estate, tailor, friends, dogs, whatever – without ever wholly displacing them. The sticking together, and not snobbishness or the fact of being well-heeled, accounts for no stories being leaked to the press about the 'royals' in their time spent in the shadow of Windsor. It may be that a shared uniform, however eccentric, minimises social differences, turning every boy into an Etonian. However, *Nigger at Eton* (1972) tells a slightly different story. Dillibe Onyeama, the son of a Nigerian judge, found himself alternately patronised by the masters, for whom he appears to have been a guinea pig testifying to Eton's powers of adaptation, or bullied:

> And so the questions did go on. 'How many maggots are there in your hair, Onyeama?'... 'Have you ever eaten human flesh?'...'Is your father a witch doctor?'... I nearly always exploded and, with sudden savagery scored with a heavy punch to the face and stomach, made a few of them cry. Their smouldering friends would go into an orgy of racial abuse shouted with the utmost hatred and bitterness.

Another African, also from Nigeria, was present at the school at the same time; and Onyeama notes that he wasn't bullied. Onyeama's torments came from the fact that he wasn't attractive or clever, and only quite good at sports. (He did bowl fast, but this was treated as evidence of racial capability.) Though no-one was tactless enough to spell out the message, Onyeama's problem came from being 'a crasher' – someone whom you might want to acknowledge in the street with a shrug, or by turning your back. In the end, he just wouldn't do.

My Etonian father-in-law, a squire-farmer intellectual to whom life, for one reason or another, had never accorded adequate recognition, used to speak of the Etonian 'worship of the bitch goddess success'. This is based on the simplest of worldly indices – marriage to the right person; a job with the right title; 'a house', as the writer Anthony Powell put it, 'with a driveway' – and one fails at one's own risk.

'I know a lot of Etonians about whom you think: "Why don't they just do something, like running an antique shop?" or "Why didn't they marry someone nice and ordinary?"' a non-Etonian friend says. 'But, no, they can't or won't. Some set of wholly ridiculous expectations remains with them, spoiling what might be otherwise comfortable lives.' I know all about such expectations. They are at once ridiculous, life-threatening and faintly touching. If they didn't exist at all, Eton would seem an intolerable place.

Etonian *noblesse oblige* isn't, to be sure, a quality shared by everyone who has attended the school. But it can be found expressed to perfection in the career of David Astor, the rich, liberal, editor-proprietor of the *Observer* newspaper from 1948 to 1975. Astor's parents were Christian Scientists (his mother, the redoubtable Nancy, teetotaller and Tory M.P., 'gave a lot of blood and drew a lot of blood' from her family; and David struggled against her long after youth, through several crack-ups). This accounts in part for the high-mindedness he displayed writing home from Eton at the age of seventeen:

Nobility undoubtedly exists but has no connection with economic position [it is] a quality of thought... and appreciation of the common good and the unselfishness and ability to minister it... [A noble person] is essentially a man of balanced character. Not an aesthete or a fanatic about anything. An enrolled man of the world.

Writing to Nancy, Astor judged his Eton career to be 'dim in the extreme' – because he was 'obscure and retiring'. In another letter, however, he contrasts himself with a similarly dubiously-equipped but poor boy. 'Here's this fellow starting from scratch,' Astor says. 'He may go far if he's very able, but the odds are a hundred to one that he'll be a dull mediocrity.' And what of Astor himself, so young and burdened? 'My position gives me a greater scope for good,' he concludes. 'You can sneer at material possessions and circumstances but their presence seems to save years of donkey-work even if it necessitates the same amount of spade work to get character.'

I ask the ex-Tory M.P. Jonathan Aitken about the prevalence of *noblesse oblige* at Eton. Does it explain the persistence of Tory Etonians, decade after decade? 'It's a part of the tradition,' Aitken explains. 'But you must add in another aristocratic streak in the school – taking risks, jumping the highest fence, gambling. Politics has always seemed like the greatest game in town. One cannot resist taking part.' However, there is a third aspect of the Etonian fascination with public life, and this, Aitken explains, consists of 'oiling'. Etonians have to compete for office within the school. They are elected not just to grand societies such as Pop, but to lowlier ones, to Debate (the association of senior boys within each house) and even, Aitken explains, to the Scientific Society. 'It breeds a certain speciality of behaviour. You know how to get elected, you know how to please.'

Aitken describes to me the art of 'oiling' as practised by Etonians. He recalls making a speech in the Debating Society in which he criticised a boy who'd been buying drinks ('socking' is the Eton word) at the school shop, Jack's, in an effort to get elected to Pop. 'I said "He's taken up painting, and he'll soon have created a masterpiece in oils to hang in Jack's." I don't know if it was funny but it got a huge roar.' But Aitken insists that there is such a thing as good, or successful, oiling. 'You have to learn how to oil,' he says. 'And at Eton, you do learn.'

***

What happens when ill-luck, changed circumstances, or maladroitness, ensure that it is no longer possible to follow the golden Eton path? I once discussed the matter of success and Etonians with the Indian writer Ved Mehta, who saw them as a caste doomed to lose status and identity. Supplying the story of an Etonian friend of his, wildly successful at school, winner of numberless awards, who killed himself once the prospects of more success were no longer available, Mehta evoked what he termed the 'coyote howl' of disaffection to be observed among Etonians.

The howling was something he claimed to find, much disguised, in me. I reacted defensively, but the question of disappointment still haunts me. Is my own periodically expressed anger about the sheer awfulness of things not some school-implanted sense of being let down? I fervently hope not. The question of what, if anything, Eton success means becomes harder to answer as the school's own systems of measurement appear more remote from those applied elsewhere. I think of how Etonians track each others' progress along invisible, highly structured timelines from which one must not have departed. Such conversations sound like the ruminations of a lost Marxist sect, or Bourbon courtiers discussing precedence half a century after the rules ceased to apply.

***

These days there is a smallish, though not insignificant, price to be paid for the privileges of Eton. Only a few decades ago, though, the rules of the game were formulated differently. In traditional Britain, now defunct, a degree of socially contrived harshness prevailed. It was believed that some sort of punishment should precede the enjoyment of privilege, tempering (or making more desirable) enjoyment, toughening the body to improve the mind – or, if you believe other historians, it was simply the case that in aristocratic houses children, like animals, were thrashed for their good.

Beating was a serious matter at Eton, and here a brief history lesson is required. For the great age of mass beatings one must go back to the stewardship of Dr. Keate, the savage disciplinarian who presided over the school as Head Master from 1810 until he retired exhausted in 1834. Keate on one occasion beat 87 boys using 40 rods, replacing them as they broke. During his regime, a series of rebellions took place, in which boys appear either to have staged protests over the punishment of individuals, which were greeted with additional chastisement, or, more frequently, to have smashed windows or broken schoolrooms to pieces. The riots were linked by contemporary observers to continental Jacobinism, though they probably had more to do with the appalling conditions of the school. In subsequent years, punishment became milder and more selective. In 1876 boys were given the right to beat other boys. (They were allowed to use stiff, knobbed, bum-scarring numbers or the swishy, whistling variety, most painful when worn with use, and split. They were not permitted to resort to the birch, a collection of twigs with thorns that could be applied to the posterior of the boy with a motion similar to that of whisking eggs – this particular weapon's use was restricted, presumably because of the degree of damage that could be done in less than practised hands, to the Head Master, or Lower Master.) All beatings, by the Head Master as well as boys, were finally forbidden in 1972.

Beatings were conducted by the Eton Society or 'Pop,' the self-electing group of prefects. A 1902 glossary, published by boys as a guide to the school, gives a copious account of the range of punishments considered appropriate. Of the Pop cane it relates, lovingly: 'For purposes of chastisement it has a peculiar sense of poignancy.' A contemporary observer remarks:

> Flogging at Eton, and the endurance of flogging, were as much a form of athletics as compulsory football. There was no sense of shame involved, and hardly any of justice and responsibility. The upper boys quite frankly enjoyed beating the lower boys, and were proud of whatever skill they possessed in doing it so as to inflict maximum pain...

For every such remark one can find, decade by decade, suggestions that punishment isn't excessive, that it doesn't do any harm, that boys will become softies if it is abolished, etc. etc. Did these bizarre practices maim generations of the English elite, or help to create a version of the Samurai class? This isn't an easy question to answer, not least because of the *sangfroid* with which such episodes are traditionally recounted. Wilfred Thesiger's autobiography, *The Life Of My Choice,* contains a typical instance of this. Thesiger, who tells us that his time at Eton was 'one of the most formative influences of (my) life,' giving him 'responsibility, the decencies of life, and standards of civilised behaviour' was, it would seem, beaten ferociously. He is at pains to distinguish between beatings which were 'fair' – and thus accepted cheerfully, no matter how painful – and those that weren't. But it's not clear what he thinks of this birching received for failing to learn Latin:

As a Lower boy at the time I came before the Lower Master. Ramsey, pompous, rubicund and white-haired, put on his mortar-board as he pronounced sentence, and then, wrapped in his gown, swept into the adjoining room where the block, dating back some two hundred years, was kept... On either side of the block stood a praepostor from the sixth form, there to see that sentence was carried out and to order. The junior praepostor bowed and handed the birch to the senior praepostor, who handed it with a bow to the Lower Master. The whole proceeding was reminiscent of a beheading at Tower Hill. After a birching, twelve shillings and sixpence was put on the bill – I presume for a new birch, but I never verified this.

We'll never know how much pain Thesiger (and the many thousands punished in this bizarre way) experienced. Nor will we be able to do more than guess how it marked them. But it is possible not wholly to despise so much detachment, indeed to admire it, and to see in it some element of the admirably impenetrable mask worn by the English ruling class in the long years of its prime.

If there are a number of accounts of Eton chastisement; however this is not the case, or at least not in the same way, with the practice of buggery, commonly regarded as synonymous with attendance at Eton. Instead, there are hazy intimations of crushes between elder and younger boys, whispered evocations of romance. As one might expect, masters were enamoured of their charges. They were more than prepared to disregard lack of hygiene at the school. In 1867, William Johnson, composer of the 'Eton Boating Song', was forced to leave the school after a scandal involving the son of the British Minister to Constantinople, and two younger boys called Chat and Brett. His surviving diaries record petting between the boys ('My arms were around him, & Elliott's were around him and me...') Johnson befriended the parents of the boys, staying with them under what any parent would now regard as suspicious circumstances. He enjoyed watching, but it is not clear from his own letters whether his interest was more than voyeuristic – or indeed aesthetic.)

It is hard to be dogmatic about the frequency of single-sex relations at Eton. Scandals are recorded decade by decade, and boys are regularly sacked for the practice of 'vice'. But it is never clear how much sex goes on between boys – whether it is performed Salo-style, as in the work of Pasolini, or, as seems more probable, fleeting and furtive.

Sex probably takes place, as it does in prisons, with the acknowledgement that it's happening because there's nothing better around. And it is thus, grudgingly, between mild guilt and self-hatred, telling themselves that they aren't queer even as they perform homosexual acts, that Etonians receive their sexual initiation.

A friend who was considered beautiful at Eton and who later admitted to his homosexuality, explains:

Eton, and other single sex schools are the worst places to discover that you are gay. Somehow most of the boys know about it – and let you know. And the masters also know, but of course they don't want to know, not really. Seduction is what you get to when you have power – and being seduced, one of course knows that, and one cannot really refuse, or not easily. It comes down to the cruellest double standard. The boy who seduces you is 'normal'. He'll end up with a wife and family and a nice house. And you? Well, nobody knows what will happen to you. Nobody cares much.

Those 'caught in the act' were usually sacked, though they were sometimes allowed to stay on for the rest of the term so that the reason for their departure could remain hidden. (Bizarrely, if a boy had been assaulted, it was at one time customary to ask his parents if they wished the perpetrator to be sacked. The parents of one aristocrat who had been violated in the showers, I recall, allowed the rapist to stay on, and he went on to assault another boy the following term.) Meanwhile, buggery was outlawed even as it was acknowledged to be unstoppable – it must simply be kept within reasonable limits.

Some insight into the deviant, self-contradictory sexual politics of Eton comes in *Stand Before Your God,* the autobiography of Peter Watkins, an American who was educated at Eton. As a prefect Watkins recalls finding two boys, one lying on a bed, the other 'wearing his tail coat and waistcoat, but his trousers were down by his ankles.' In an effort to appear conscientious, he told the head prefect of his house, who went with him to report the offence to the House Master. But the House Master chose not to punish the offenders – and the prefect let it be known that it was Watkins who had informed on the boys. In consequence Watkins was ostracised, objects were stolen from him. This treatment continued until he apologised – not to the boys whom he interrupted, of course, but to his friends who enjoyed their own, illicit relationships. 'I don't blame you,' he said. 'It was a terrible mistake, and there was nothing I can do to put it right, and I won't be forgiving myself.' After that, he was forgiven.

'I never masturbated at Eton,' Lord Longford tells us elsewhere; 'it never occurred to me... one boy made an advance to me, but only once.' His experience would appear to be out of the ordinary. 'The amount of masturbation was terrific,' the writer Adam Nicolson recalls. 'And the sexual ignorance was terrific, unless you happened be the sort of boy lucky enough to have a louche sort of life in London. Perfectly unconsciously, one came to think that there were people in the world – and then there were girls about whom one knew nothing. And this went on for some time after I had left the school.' I'm surprised to find even the super-urbane, floral-shirted Johnnie Boden saying the same thing. 'I most regret the single sex thing,' he says. 'It really held me back.'

***

Others have a darker memory of sexual confinement. The film critic Derek Malcolm describes 'a homosexual society, a pederastic society':

Another moment (I experienced) was eating some apple crumble in the house dining room – the apple crumble was delicious – and I can remember a beautiful boy, with the most beautiful bum in bumfreezers, going up to ask for a second helping... I was eating the crumble and thinking what bliss to be eating the crumble and going to bed with him at the same time. And I don't think I will ever forget those moments... I just wish that any hetero relationship that I've had since had measured up, and I don't think they do because at sixteen everything is so fresh and intense.

'Homosexuality,' Cyril Connolly wrote in 1938 in his autobiographical memoir *Enemies of Promise,* 'was the forbidden tree around which our little Eden dizzyingly revolved.' In the same book, he wrote of the British elite as being 'cowardly, and in the last resort homosexual'. I have never been quite sure how to interpret this passage. It seems unlikely that Connolly believes that buggery was practised throughout the British elite. Instead he appears to be alluding to the gaucheness and lovelessness that comes from being immured without women, and the way it translates, later in life, into a number of serious social or erotic disorders, among them a disposition to hang out with men like yourself, keeping women at a chilly distance. There must be many hundreds of Eton lives, in which both mothers and wives appear shadows beside the company of other men, in particular those whom one has known in adolescence. Perhaps Connolly is right in defining such attitudes as a form of homosexuality.

Many Etonians over the years were caught supplementing the fitful sexual practices that appear to characterise the British posh class with acts of buggery (often committed with Guardsmen) in St. James Park; and it is hard not to see this as a school inheritance. Alongside the bluff, man-to-man intercourse of Old Etonians, a secondary, campy idiom persists. 'Did I sleep with you?' is an opening remark of one Etonian I meet. 'I slept with so many people that I've forgotten who was who.' Meanwhile, the school history coyly draws attention to the change, post-1960s, caused by the availability of 'teenage girls who had previously been restrained from early sexual adventure, and had tended to be more interested in older males.'

One effect of sexual liberation on Etonians, it would seem to the history's author Timothy Card, a bachelor Etonian who taught at Eton for 50 years, is, regrettably, 'an excessive horror of homosexuality'. It seems that Etonians are bad around gays – locked up together for centuries, they haven't wholly adopted precepts of correctness. A parent I know bemoans this lack of tolerance. 'Now they get out more, and see girls more easily, the boys are truly homophobic,' he says.

One can legitimately pose the same question about buggery as about beating – would the history of the British elite have been different if Eton and places like it (though for some reason the cultural tag of buggery is stronger around Eton than, say, rivals such as Winchester or Harrow) had not been single sex schools? I've met many girls, and later women, who are convinced that Etonians are almost all homosexual, but who, for this reason, find them attractive. Shyness and arrogance go together in Etonians, they say, a bit thrilled. This makes Etonians exciting, ripe for seduction. 'They're so up themselves,' a teenage girl tells me graphically. One woman I meet keeps a tally of bagged Etonians in the style of Lord Byron stuffing a cushion with the pubic hair of his conquests. When I suggest that such behaviour might be considered bizarre if not perverse, she laughs. 'I wish I'd gone there,' she says. 'Think of the wonderful clothes. Think of all those boys.'

Plainly, the sexuality of Etonians has generated its quota of orally-transmitted legends. 'I think I might be gay if I hadn't met her,' is how a young Etonian whom I meet for the first time in a crowded London restaurant speaks of the woman seated beside him, whom he intends to wed. I wonder whether this is silly, or merely charming – the stuff of an unusual wedding-day address, perhaps. But the young man appears to be in earnest. I want to ask the couple whether they, too, will send their son to Eton. And then I recall a passage from a novel describing a 'dark, handsome, boy from whom pent-up energy rises almost dangerously':

> Add to this the peculiar odour, strong but not unpleas-
> ant, which I'd come to associate with Etonians (the
> smell of infrequently washed adolescents in formal
> clothes)... How the way he moved, the checked speed
> and intensity, the hectic flushes and sudden gestures
> expressed him: rapt feverish, intellectual, nothing vul-
> gar, nothing shabby (except, of course, the clothes,
> threadbare, Spartan, and redolent, among other things,
> of virtue.)

This is from a novel written by a woman to whom I was
once married, written just before death, in what appears to
have been a paroxysm of recollection. It describes, only a
little fancifully, myself aged 19.

'What he knows so far are the expensively procured abus-
es of public school,' she continues, 'the brute assaults of the
elders, the idealisation (and fear) of the off-limits female
world outside.'

Is there really such a thing as Eton sexuality, narcissistic,
touchingly needy as well as aggressive? We are, all of us, prepared to do anything to attract the attention of those whom
we love, and maybe so much profusely expelled Eton charm
and energy was no more than a banal come-on. But I can

conclude, too, that there are inventions that become real enough, and that Eton, with all its myths, is one of them. Describing a hall of distorting mirrors, I know that it was all real for me – I don't have to ask what Eton made of me, because I know already. And I am sure that all Etonians feel the same.

CHAPTER FOUR

B eing Eton starts not with the first interviews, the exam results or measuring up of trousers, but the day you arrive. Eton becomes, generically, 'school.' It's the only place to be. Absurd though it may sound, it is just like that – the shock, which never wholly wore off, of finding out that one's own life matters.

I'd been sick for the first month of the new school year, and when I sat down in my room and tried over-eagerly to do my first day's homework, a boy came in. He appeared minuscule, Munchkin-size, in steel-rimmed specs, wearing the highly unflattering Eton jacket and stiff, ink-stained, Pierrot collar on which his small chin was hooked upwards, making him seem still frailer. He seemed burdened, sinking under some weight. I asked him about lessons, and he faltered, his voice piping with fear. 'I can keep up if I work terribly hard,' he said. 'but it's awfully difficult.' Then he smiled, revealing misshapen teeth and an elaborate effort at dental correction. His duty was to coach me for what he explained was the extremely difficult examination awaiting me in two weeks' time, filled with geographical and linguistic teasers. 'I only got through on my third time,' he says. 'But we've heard you're awfully keen. There's no doubt that you'll be alright. Everyone says so.'

The notion of keenness – the word is enunciated with reprobation as well as envy – is my first introduction to Eton slang. I become familiar with the following terms and usages. A 'half' is a term, though in fact there are three of these, as at any other school. A 'fag' is a young boy who runs errands for older ones – there are no sexual connotations. The word 'tug' is from the dog Latin 'gens togata', and a tug (snobbery comes imprinted within the dog latin) is one of the 70 King's Collegers, most of whose fees are paid for, and who are segregated in the older buildings of the school. They are usually more intelligent than the rest of the school, also reputedly cliquish, though this is not so, as I rapidly discover. 'Oppidans' (more dog Latin – the word means 'townies') make up the rest of the school. There are 1220 Oppidans, fully fee-paying (though this would later change), grouped in houses through the town. Being boring, I rapidly learn, is the worst sin at Eton. Not ever being too serious, is at the core of the school style, and I try to master this, becoming adept in banter.

At first encounter, Eton argot appears overwhelming. A 'Dame' is a female, usually of august appearance (in my own case snobbish and apparently descended from Lord Byron, 'the size of a mountain, with hair all over her chin and face, and warts everywhere,' as another former charge describes her) who assists the House Master with the running of the house. The happily named Boys' Maids do beds in the morning, thus creating in every Etonian a lifelong craving to live in a hotel, or service apartment – a persistent Eton myth tells how X or Y (an especially unscrupulous, randy boy) had sex Bond-style with a Boys' Maid, but so far as I can tell this has no basis in reality. Homosexuals (as distinct from boys who think of themselves as heterosexual but have sex with other boys, of whom there appear to be many) are 'batty.' A 'burry' comes from the French. meaning 'bureau', or a desk, and these are rickety, crammed with papers. A 'div' is a class period. A 'tear' is a piece of work so bad that it is returned with a rip down the middle – one has to hand these to the House Master and receive a talking-to, though, being excessively, boringly diligent, I never receive any of these. Being 'flogged' means being beaten by the Head Master or Lower Master with a birch, whereas being beaten merely means being caned by another boy, at the approval of the House Master. (Boys are present when a master flogs a boy; but, for some reason I cannot fathom, boys may beat each other without the presence of an adult.) Being in 'Pop' involves being elected to a society whose members can wear coloured waistcoats, with braid on the edge of their tail coats. The best thing in Eton, in life indeed, is to have been elected a member of Pop – near-grown boys pine for the honour, and those who narrowly miss Pop are said never to recover, going through life as if they were second best. Should I think of myself as Pop material, I wonder. Prudently, I decide this would be a mistake. I don't know yet who I am in the Etonian scheme of things, and it's not good for me to set my sights too high.

Next there are 'dry-bobs', 'wet bobs' and 'slack bobs' – meaning boys who play cricket, row, or do no sports at all. An array of caps and colours, awesome in their complexity and the nuance with which they express obscure sports usually played only by Etonians, is brought to my consciousness. They come back to me each evening in my sleep. Finally, I stand in front of four older boys, Prefects; the room they occupy, known as 'the Library', contains no books, only yellowing pin-ups. My inquisitors are seated in ancient, stained armchairs.

What is brown-and-magenta with a slim line? My own

house – good. And what is purple-and-white? College, I think. Yes. But what are Eton Fives? Not a mysterious tea ritual, but a sport played with a glove against a laboriously reconstructed replica of a portion of Chapel steps. And, now, what is the Eton Field Game? I have played the game, hating it; but I can at least recall the rules. Good. And what is a 'scug'? I pause here, and I remember – a scug is some-one with no sporting distinction: i.e. with the right to wear

A wet-bob's collection of hats, 1937

no cap other than the dark blue and light blue one that I have been given. Passing without difficulty, I am happy. I walk back from the Library.

Meanwhile, I learn that nicknames are handed out to everyone. My House Master is called Mr. How – a misfortune that leads later to his caricature (the actor didn't have a speaking role) on the West End stage. This paper-dry, 60-something, tobacco-breath virgin, who presides ineffectually over M'Tutors, is for some reason, perhaps because it is so inappropriate, called 'Oily'.

Without excessive originality, the current Headmaster is known as 'Red Robert' Birley, but his successor, name of Anthony Chenevix- Trench, will be called 'Chummy,' or, more picturesquely, 'Chauvinist Stench'. (A toe-curling Stalkyesque humour persists, at odds with the grand ethos of the school; and later, I find out that Douglas Hurd was known among Foreign Office juniors as 'Hitler' Hurd – because he beat boys enthusiastically when at Eton.) Boys are called 'Wee A', 'Reeders', 'Tarty', 'Jockstrap' – anything at all. I am known as 'Froggy' for a bit (because my mother is French) but, presumably because it isn't specially funny, this is allowed to lapse. I am relieved to have no nickname.

When I go for a pee (the toilets are heated and, as had not been the case in the previous educational establishment I had been to, close to my room), a very large ugly boy

101

plastered in aftershave, with his hair brilliantined in what I come to recognise as the scent of limes from Trumper's of Jermyn Street, a reddish splotch on his shirt, looks at my open pyjama top, and asks if I think I am sexy. When I say no, not specially – or something like that – he giggles. I don't imagine he is appraising me, because I am skinny, already very tall; but he opens my pyjama bottoms, looks at my penis, and smiles. I am not excessively upset by this. Something tells me that I will be lucky, never having to try too hard to fend off unwanted attentions. I am not entirely right about this, but for the moment I am content to be left alone.

True Etonians – those whose family have attended the school for many generations – probably don't notice they are at Eton at all. Their lives at school are a prelude to experiencing the emotion of having been there, as nostalgia. This is what the Eton Boating Song tells us:

We'll recollect our races,
We'll to the flag be true
And youth will be still in our faces
When we cheer for the Eton crew

I can see boys around me who will fulfil this sublimely unthinking vision of life. I know that this is not for me. But there are others, lodged in College – sons of professors, quiet boys tucked in the corner of form, Greeks, high-caste Indians or Jews (Africans and Arabs will come later, but not, it seems, British blacks) – for whom the school already means something different. I can sense already that so large a place in fact contains many different schools. At the bottom, struggling in class and barely taught, are the no-hopers, those content not to work at all – a minority, mostly coming from insouciant county families. There are fewer of these each year. Somewhere in the middle are the majority, never excessively stirred or shaken, but respectably taught, fitted out for life, and perhaps even a spell at University (Christ Church, Oxford, or King's, Cambridge, though this, too, has changed). These are the very nice, very civilised, impeccably easy-going Etonians, and it is with them that I make tea – this is called 'messing', appropriately, consisting of fried eggs, sausages, tomatoes, bacon and fried bread – and it compensates for the disgusting house food. Fagging errands are assigned at teatime, by ringing a bell; and I acquire a lifelong habit of eating rapidly, head over the plate, defying indigestion, so as to be ready if summoned. I learn quickly about the boys who are my age. Having 'side' – i.e. boasting about any degree of success – isn't held to be good form. But I discover that if I help them with their work I won't be called a swot.

It is easy to establish how one may acquire this or that cap for games, even if, as is the case with myself, one will never get them. Academic excellence at Eton, though, is more difficult to anticipate. Already it occurs to me that this quality may not depend solely on good marks, but consist of other qualities. I begin to understand that cleverness may be defined in a variety of ways, as wit, as oddness, as *savoir faire*, even as the ability to remain silent when others are talking. And cleverness is what Eton prizes, most of all. There are already boys to whom the notion is attached, and I envy them vaguely as I serve mediocre fried eggs for those to whom I have been assigned as a fag. I think of them while I am running, carrying the folded up notes (they are never sealed, and presumably this is another school custom) entrusted to me by my elders – assignments to play Fives at such and such a times, or information that the sender has received a letter from the recipient's sister. I will never amount to anything at games, and I have no conspicuous society attachments. My French half-sisters are far too old for any Etonian I might know, and we don't hang out with aristocrats. It occurs to me that, if I am to amount to anything, I must think of learning something.

But I can be happy here, taking pleasure from schoolboy jokes, never excessively pushing myself and constructing a self that is pleasing partly because I know it won't last. We do teasing, myself and my friends. We behave like the little gents we are supposed to be. I feel I am truly hopeless at organized games (so I prefer not to try) and nobody seems to care. Why should they? In accounts of school life, I am now struck by the utter absence of any references to team spirit, playing or working together etc. It isn't desirable under any circumstances to conform. Take this account of arrival from the shelf loads of school memoirs, set in the 1930s:

Never will the new boy feel so good again as when he looks on his Eton room for the first time. He has said goodbye forever to the bleak cubicle or dormitory which has hitherto been thought good enough to house him. For it is all so minute, with the roof almost touching the floor, at the corners, and a beam cutting it in two, it seems nothing short of princely. Here he will eat, sleep, work, rag, read, sing and play the fool with his friends for many months to come. Later, he will grow out of this room, and into a bigger one, more befitting his rank and station; until finally he will scorn to sit in his own room at all, preferring to lord it in the Library with the great ones.

Sitting in my room each evening, I, too, experience a

kind of wonder that I am here. Fingering a pen, inserting a stud into the ridiculous stiff collars, fighting to erase an obscure stain from the musty-smelling tail coat (how is it that even after their weekly return from the laundry, bundled up, dumped on the ledges on each landing of the tall, thin house, these coats and striped trousers smell so vile?) I summarise what I have hitherto learnt about my own life. I know that my small family live comfortably but relatively modestly in bourgeois South Kensington – there are no long driveways where we come from. My mother is French, and beautiful. She has never understood the British desire to send small boys away to school. It is my half-sisters who are permitted to go to the French Lycée in London. My mother worries about my being melancholy, and not fitting in. I know already that I will be alright. By contrast, my coming to Eton has made my gruff, shy, businessman father very happy. He was educated at what he always considers to be a lesser, though not a 'minor' public school. In some mysterious respect, judged as an induction into the right British class, my father's education proved less than satisfactory. I am to be his answer to the system which failed him. I do not know what this means, or indeed whether this will be alright for me. For the moment I am biding my time, trying to understand simple things.

***

Several decades on, I see something of this early Eton self in the first class that I re-attend. Here, twenty fifteen-year-olds examine me discreetly, wondering what I am doing as they slouch outside the schoolroom. They are here for the first scene of *The Tempest,* and a young master makes them climb up on a semicircle of benches. First they make storm noises, then, line by line, they attempt to extract meaning from Shakespeare. Patiently, the master explains what it all means:

The sky, it seems, would pour down stinking pitch,
But that the sea, mounting to the welkin's cheek,
Dashes the fire out. O I have suffered
With those that I saw suffer.

Can one really watch something – a play, for instance, but more importantly life around oneself – and suffer with those whom one observes? Is life really like that? Perhaps because it's a summer morning, Prospero's magic seems hard work. It's easier to ask the boys how much back information is smuggled into the text by the bard. Think of gossip as an aspect of the Shakespearian *oeuvre*. The boys get off their benches, and begin to decipher Shakespeare as a newspaper article. Soon they are busy constructing an alternative *Tempest* out of all the bits that have been left out. I follow them through early adolescence, dreamily unperturbed, all of them as marooned in themselves as Miranda.

Between classes, boys stroll from one classroom to another in an unhurried way, as if on their way to social engagements. The atmosphere is calm – there's none of the ragging that can be discerned at the gates of any lycée. This is where standards are maintained – one can pause, greet half-friends, snub the uncertain or grovel before the powerful. In the days I am here I get to understand, once again, the skilled, half-attentiveness inculcated at this place. You don't need to tune in all the time – it's more elegant if you don't, and beaks prefer it that way. But they will want you to exhibit the appearance of alertness at the right moment.

At Chambers, to which the Head Master takes me, and where staff exchange notes in the cavernous, panelled school hall, I notice the variety of intensely polished shoes, the posh and not so posh suits of the staff, with the odd clerical-looking cream linen jacket worn in the style of *The Importance of Being Earnest*. Beaks are oddly formal, without quite seeming old-fashioned. They stroll awkwardly towards the Head Master, and halt, bowing slightly from the waist. In small groups they appear to be conducting business like the elders of some long lost city state mysteriously conserved, a minor Venice perhaps, or a place narrowly missed by Gulliver on his travels. The people in this room appear both removed and deeply worldly. There is an archness here, which others might find archaic, or affected; and which I might once have despised. But I feel that I know enough about the world beyond Eton not to find these qualities wholly ridiculous.

It is the long sleep of early adolescence that stays with me as I am kept suspended in this strange Eton element. Doesn't all this false adulthood flatter the young into believing that they are grown up, all the while making sure that they remain incomplete? I think of this later, going through the crowded schedule of Etonians with a young economics beak, looking at the school's websites. You can try hard enough to be swept along, and the oddest things will appear normal. And so it is indeed with the busy rituals of Eton. I wish that life itself could be conducted in this way, until I realise that, for many of those with whom I was at school, it probably has been. An Eton day consists of fixed classroom moments of silence, with a drone here or there, or the scraping of feet, punctuated by the scraping of desks. Sitting in sunlight, I recall one of the moments that finally woke me up.

***

There's nothing special about this first transformation, which indeed resembles the experiences of friends who encountered bright and diligent teachers at their grammar schools or comprehensives. When I specialise at the age of sixteen – French, English, German and History are my choices – I am sent off, as the system prescribes, for tutorials in a small group with a youngish Welsh beak. I am intimidated by his cramped study, filled with books, and the long monologues occasionally interrupted by books thrown across the room.

Ray Parry loves history as a grand abstraction, and for the grand procession of characters that pass across its stage. 'You might read this,' he shouts; and then, 'Definitely this, try this.' When I tell him that some of these books appear unreadable, he throws more of them in my direction. My first two essays elicit no more than grunts. The third isn't longer, and I haven't spent more time on it – it just feels better. And so, indeed, it appears to Mr. Parry, who waves it like a baton, throwing more books in my direction. Do I want to do well? I could do well, he says. I could even get a scholarship. Of course, he says that I will have to work hard, but I can see, too, that something else is required. I will now have to be someone. I walk back to my cherished room. As usual, the house is vaguely menacing. But I now have a reason to steer past the bullying, the net of single sex couplings, the socio-sexual patronage of younger boys. I have good reason at last to evade all the sporting assignments where my performance is mediocre.

Already I think of how I have nothing to say to my father, how I cannot read his letters with any pleasure. What will I do when my father lags so far behind me? By agreement with my French grandmother, I write her a letter each week, and it returns scarred with her familiar red pencil and decorated with spidery writing. My subjunctive improves steadily. Now I ask her for books from Paris, and these come badly packed, festooned with her young girl annotations. She wants me to know about literature, so she sends me copies of André Gide, the notorious polemical gay writer and advocate of homosexual liberation, because, as she informs me, 'he wrote so well about adolescence.' To begin with, the writer's stringy lyricism has no effect on me. Then I'm amazed to read about his sexual encounters with Arab boys. Ironically my grandmother is so prudish that she sent home one of the English girls staying with her in Paris to learn French, because the latter sent a postcard bearing a fig leaf with an innocuous inscription underneath. I think of the pairings-off going on upstairs. Tarts are what desirable boys are called here. I get pestered; instead I choose to masturbate. This cannot really be what my grandmother has in mind.

Week by week, I'm given more books, which I read and annotate, even when they appear boring or badly written. Am I really as promising a pupil as I appear to be? It's not possible for me to wholly dislike this second Etonian self of mine. True, I'm wilful, arrogant, brooding. But I'm impassioned now, sitting reading in my mother's kitchen, or walking up to the park and scribbling annotations. I must know more, I tell myself. If I do, I will be someone.

***

How good is an Eton education? For the first 300 years of Eton it appears to have consisted of the most monotonous mugging up of Greek and Latin texts ('construe' was the word given to this mindless rote) with the odd patch of maths, Ancient History or French thrown in (not that the latter was ever encouraged – one Head Master even suggesting that its excessive valuation would only give an unfair advantage to boys whose fathers had French mistresses). Perhaps the classes with which House Masters supplemented the meagre amounts they made from charging for board were more inspired, but this seems doubtful. Eton retained its chaotic origins long after other schools had contrived to reform themselves. In 1860 an anonymous paterfamilias wrote this letter to *Cornhill* magazine:

Of all the public schools of England, it is the one at which the British parent pays the most for the education, and from which he receives the smallest educational return for his money. The great majority of Eton boys are stated to lead easy pleasant lives spending their time chiefly in the playing-fields and on the river, and not a little of it in the public-houses and taps of the neighbourhood, and if they are so minded, but not otherwise, acquiring a faint smattering of the classics in the intervals of play.

Boys in Rowlands: the school 'tuck shop'

But even by that stage the school, almost unbeknownst to itself, had created a countervailing system in its midst. Not all Etonians were dim or lazy; and most of the 70 Collegers certainly were not. Entry to College was competitive, and boys were graded according to their success in the examinations, and re-graded each year.

By 1900, nothing in the world could touch the elite end of Eton education. The Colleger John Maynard Keynes was urged to abandon classics in favour of mathematics; but he decided to do both. Keynes won ten prizes in his first year, eighteen in his second, eleven in his third: a total of 63 books in all. He won all the school's maths prizes. He became what his biographer Robert Skidelsky calls a 'precisian', filling letters with details of numbers of books read, numbers of lines in major poems, hours worked per day. On July 29, 1900, he recorded 'covering sixteen pages of History' in the hour and a half allotted for the examination. 'I have never accomplished more than fifteen before,' he added. But Keynes also played the Wall Game with what appears to be pleasure, and he spoke in the College Debating Society. Despite his opposition to the Boer War, he proved to be a staunch defender of British Imperialism. It was at Eton that Keynes first read Burke (a speech he made consisted of an excerpt from Burke's panegyric on Charles James Fox) and it is astonishing to see how many of his latter-day attitudes were already in place when he was at the school. This is how he described 'true' Liberalism in a 'College Pop' debate, aged seventeen:

> It is not root and branch reform, it is not the exaltation of the ignorant at the expense of the privileged. It is the spirit that frankly faces the current evils... and makes a statesmanlike commonsense effort to correct them. It is, as far as possible, free from prejudice; it is always desirous to probe and investigate... it will accept things as they are and practise what is noble so long as it is consistent with what is practicable.

Indeed Keynes is said to have been promiscuous in College, signalling successful seductions with notches in panelling. Of course, his letters home make no mention of this. Instead, they chronicle the extreme stress of this pressured, hothouse style of education. Crack-ups in College were not infrequent, and many boys appeared not to recover from stress. It is thought that Harold Macmillan had to be removed from College as a result of overwork (though others allege that the real reason was homosexuality). By contrast with those of Oppidans, College memoirs are dourly over-achieving, a story not of batting successes but of grind and prizes. It is surprising how many non-games players – the slight philosopher-to-be A.J. Ayer and even the gangly George Orwell – muddied and bruised themselves at the Wall.

Some observers suppose that the existence of 70 less-rich Collegers within the school transformed Eton into a microcosm of the British class system, but this is something of an exaggeration. Collegers had their fees paid, but they had to have acquired a classical education of sorts at a fee-paying preparatory school. This meant that they couldn't be from poor families. 'The hostility which was generally supposed to exist between Collegers and Oppidans... cannot be explained on Marxist lines,' the school history informs us sagely. 'Rather, it is a matter for the anthropologist.' Collegers came from what would now be regarded as more or less comfortably off, middle or upper-middle class, non-aristocratic, even suburban families. But College did come to fulfil a primitive role of social engineering. A pace-setter within the school, its function nationally was to supply intelligence to the English elite in just the right proportions.

To put it most crudely, Collegers were at Eton to acquire an education, but also, as Matthew Arnold expressed it, to 'civilise our gentlemen'. In 1910 visiting inspectors congratulated Eton for 'educating boys whose circumstances make it difficult or impossible for the school work to be as important in their eyes as it is in the eyes of less fortunate schoolboys.' In true English style, this ad hoc arrangement was judged to be mutually beneficial. Collegers were supposed to draw sustenance from the proximity of richer, idler aristocratic boys, acquiring *savoir faire*. Such contradictions within the school became part of its folklore. You could be highly intelligent, like a Colleger, but you were unlikely also to be rich. Charm was always important, but the intelligent were likely to be less charming. (The most intelligent, like Keynes, weren't charming at all; but this didn't really matter.) Only the happiest few — Eton sanctified their memory by encouraging them to return to their scene of their triumphs, ritually placing their offspring in their tracks when the time came — were both wholly charming and utterly intelligent.

So the school lived on, a grand upper class mansion of a place, hopelessly ramshackle in some places, brutally efficient elsewhere, in which many things, some of them contradictory, or nefarious, could take place in apparent harmony, with a coherent purpose. But no good thing can last forever, even at Eton, and by the 1950s the school tradition had begun to look distinctly frayed. Then the school acquired a new Head Master, Robert Birley, who had reformed the post-war German educational system, restoring the notion of academic independence to a university system worn to nothingness by collusion with Nazism.

Flat-footed, vague in manner, with a huge voice and watery pale Eton-blue eyes, Birley antagonised many parents with his liberal, or even socialist views. But he remained a devout Anglican, a traditionalist who presided over the restoration of the Chapel, choosing the parables and miracles in John Piper's windows. He never knew the names of most of the boys in his charge, and it would not have occurred to him that this was important. Instead he gave grandiose sermons in which he castigated practitioners of apartheid with the aid of citations from Toynbee.

Birley understood that within Eton one must always do things slowly. From the early 1950s onwards, motivated by a hard-headed consideration of changed fortunes, he began to lay stress on intelligence. No longer could Eton assume that its pupils would have automatic access to places at Oxford and Cambridge. It wasn't enough to be exotic or superior. Belatedly, Eton adjusted to the existence of the 1944 Education Act, introducing A levels and confronting the phenomenon of grammar school excellence. Change came very slowly – with 60 per cent of boys coming from Old Etonian families, and nearly half of its housemasters educated at Eton, the school remained recognisably tied to its nobly amateurish past. In Birley's time the two Etons – one bright, somewhat neurotic and over-achieving, the other definitively laid back, sluggishly retrograde –

remained in contrast to each other.

I can remember Birley very clearly, as a distant somewhat intimidating figure, who inscribed the prizes I won and made speeches that appalled my businessman father. But it is Birley's successor, Anthony Chenevix-Trench, whom I recall best, not wholly with pleasure. He was smallish, physically unimpressive and with a faint voice. Although his record was said to be impeccable, there was nothing special about his classical teaching, or indeed his rambling, dull sermons, and one must assume that he was chosen because he seemed modern, and didn't always wear a cassock.

What the boys rapidly understood, even if their elders did not, was that much was wrong with 'Chummy', as the boys called him. Chenevix-Trench had no previous connection with Eton. He was a classical scholar, who had first read Herodotus at the age of seven, and, in his unassuming way, a brave man. He had been starved and, it would seem, tortured in a Japanese camp, where he kept himself alive while breaking rocks by translating A.E. Houseman's *A Shropshire Lad* into Latin from memory. But he was also, famously, an exponent, even an addict, of corporal punishment, and a closet drinker. Believing that boys should be beaten, he preferred to do this in private – breaking with the Eton tradition whereby boys were present each time the Head Master beat anyone. Where Birley had refrained from excessive 'flogging', his successor relished it – 'a good thing the N.S.P.C.C. do not know about it', he remarked once.

Chenevix-Trench failed dismally at Eton, ruining his career; and he was finally 'asked to leave' in 1970, though his dismissal ultimately was as much a consequence of his inability to make up his mind as for the beatings. His not so hidden penchant came to light long after his death, with the 1994 publication of the school history. Had those who appointed Chenevix-Trench known about his *faiblesses*, and chosen to disregard them? Why had they done so? No-one gave a satisfactory answer – and there were of course many Old Etonians ready to come forward and declare that they had been made into men by these bizarre practices. But there was something really odd about Chummy. As the journalist Paul Foot, a pupil at Shrewsbury when Chenevix-Trench was headmaster there, was able to point out, 'the sensuous fingering of his pupils' buttocks before and after the interminable beatings' usually went with 'profuse, lachrymose expressions of friendship'.

And yet it was Chummy, improbably, who stood for change. 'I believe I have met a prophet,' said Vincent Mulchrome of the *Daily Mail*.

'Eton will not be Eton any more by the time I leave,' Trench told the *Daily Express* gossip column William Hickey, suggesting the school might be turned into a sixth- form college for those lacking a neighbourhood grammar school of real quality. He was wrong about this, of course – but by the mid-1960s all boys at Eton were receiving a real education, increasing the proportion of its pupils who went to Oxford and Cambridge. Under Trench, Eton half-successfully modernised itself. Without knowing it, I was a beneficiary of these efforts – I was to be a riposte to the existence of bright grammar school boys, perhaps, or even an attempt to recreate Eton in their non-toff image. And in this respect I suppose I am indebted to him.

***

Another classroom I visit contains a smaller number of sixteen-year-olds revising for A levels. The subject is 1066, and all of them know enough to score high marks on Harold, the arrow, and so on. The teaching focuses on the question of what historical sources are to be believed, and why. We are asked to consider no less than four separate accounts of the battle, each of them in some respects less than plausible. Is it possible to make out the truth from these accounts? Does this matter? Something of the intensity of my own obsession with history as a teenager returns to me. I really was interested in events such as the historiography of the French Revolution, or endless arguments of rival schools of historians about the role of the 'gentry', defined as a prototypical middle class, in the overthrow of King Charles I. Could one really ever know anything real about the past – and indeed about the present? These are questions that still bother me.

I go next to a seminar given by Dr. Jane Grant, head of the History department, in the comfortable surroundings of the Marten Library. Ms. Grant is blonde, nicely dressed, with a crisp Ulster accent. Here are boys about to go to Oxford and Cambridge, but it is clear that Ms. Grant doesn't worry about such trifles as examinations. The piece of paper I am given surveys 50-odd years of labour legislation in the United States. It poses the question: Why did the U.S. not evolve in the same direction as European states – or, to put it in a simpler way, how is it that America stacks so much in favour of employers, defining capitalism in a fashion that favours shareholders rather than workers? Much of this, Ms. Grant points out, can be attributed to the fact that property rights are enshrined in the United States Constitution as it is interpreted by the usually conservative Supreme Court. However, it would be a mistake to assume that things were ever quite so simple – other factors come into play, such as the state of public opinion, views expressed in the press, or indeed the fact that American society is fundamentally different from its European equivalents, founded for a distinct purpose, and composed of waves of immigrants for whom mobility and getting on in life are lasting goals.

I sit through more than an hour of discussion featuring half-forgotten players in American history such as the I.W.W. – the Wobblies, as the union was called – and pieces of legislation as difficult to digest as the Sherman anti-trust act. The boys are deferential, polite, rarely disagreeing with their politely brutal teacher, and sometimes I feel I am sitting through a replica of one of Mrs. Thatcher's cabinet meetings. How many people in Britain remember when Walter Reuther of the United Auto Workers first got companies to open their books? How many even now would be capable of analysing the implications of President Reagan's impulsive locking out of air controllers? By the time we have begun to consider such factors as the effect of boom-and-bust on unionisation, and the impact of ethnic diversity – the ceaseless flow of immigrants and internal migrants – my head is spinning. The boys appear attentive, unfazed by the sweep of this argument or the detail. It occurs to me that they won't be asked to approach any subject in this way for some years even at university. Maybe this is the best they will ever get in life – unless they are able to circumvent what is offered to them, making their own way.

I walk back through the small throng of Etonians, with

a sense of rapture I'd forgotten. But something is wrong, too, and I find that I recapture the wrongness as I write. Maybe this kind of education, which I have, by and large, tried to live by, isn't right. Maybe an experience can be so good that it ends by losing its original function, becoming something distinctly less appealing. I try to explain this to friends, and fail. But the feeling of inappositeness returns when I talk to the writer Adam Nicolson. He recalls an Eton beak who experimented in 'de-Platonisation' – this meant going with his pupils to the local playground, getting on the swings and shedding what the beak called 'the high-flying, over-intellectualised life of the imagination'. Nicolson thinks that this saved his skin. 'I was brought to a pitch of great intellectual sophistication at Eton,' he recalls. 'But it was no more than a crust. There was a vacuum of understanding of people in the world. I had all the analytical equipment I needed, and more. But I didn't really understand anything.' I ask what happened to the beak on the swings. 'Oh, he was fired,' Nicolson says. 'They got rid of him quickly.'

CHAPTER FIVE

One summer evening I attend a school performance of *The Merchant of Venice*. The production is rich, with good costumes, wigs, plausible Venetian props. This isn't a play I like, and I am huffily irritated by the spectacle of young rich boys impersonating anti-Semites, and not wholly convinced by a seventeen-year-old Shylock in fake dreadlocks and a glued-on beard. Typically, what the programme calls 'incorrectness' is played up as if it wasn't bigotry, and the play's highly unattractive characters treated as if they and their views were normal. I reflect that this must have something to do with the privilege of Eton. But I soon see my impatience for what it is – the performance suffers from being an expression of the frustration of being at once young and powerless, but also over-able.

These young actors are being made to try too hard – and I am required to evaluate what they are doing as if it might be touched with genius.

In the dusk I listen to parents as they point out the actress Penelope Keith, congratulating each other on the quality of the performances of their offspring. It's difficult to be so favoured, so absolutely on-the-nail brilliant. I recall the stories of adolescent disillusionment that litter English life and letters. From Dickens' Pip through L.P. Hartley's *Go Between*, they recount lucklessness with an odd and wholly English relish. It's never clear whether in England being spoilt is a cause of downfall, or merely something that one can never avoid paying for. But promise is celebrated only to be destroyed. Good fortune, looks, intelligence – all become part of failure. Finally, the protagonist succumbs to humiliation or, more usually, fails to grow out of the glories of the playing field – one way or another, he passes into the safe, defeated anonymity of middle age. These stories can be told about Eton, too, but they are given an extra twist by a more complicated notion of success. It isn't enough to be good at this, or that – here one has to be special in different ways. So perhaps the fall, or the disillusionment, is proportionately greater.

These days, when teenage boys are imagined to fail in relation to their cooler, less messed up sisters, the facts of growing up have been reduced to a set of symptoms: pimples, attention deficit, and so on. I do recall some splendour in being young, most of all the moment when I could begin to think that I might be attractive to others. At least, though this isn't quite the same thing, I could feel important.

I discover a forgotten videotape in the BBC library entitled 'Eton 1965'. In black-and-white film what appears to be a 1965 day at Eton (though the film was shot over many months, stitched together out of set pieces) is recreated. I can see myself, briefly, in the dark images, walking onto Chapel, standing to one side. Many of those whom I have known and forgotten acquire posthumous existence for me. Here is a Jewish friend whose family ran a camera shop in Baker Street. Here, addressing fellow-prefects on what appeared to be his favourite topic of the time – the wearing of striped socks – is the President of Pop, William Waldegrave, later a Tory M.P. and Minister. And here is the Captain of the School, Aidan Foster-Carter, whose articles about North Korea I sometimes read – of course he is speaking about the Vietnam War, to which he was implacably opposed, almost alone at Eton, and sometime before the cause became fashionable. Here, dressed in stick-ups and already looking a little plump, is the boy for whom I am searching. He's standing outside the Head Master's chamber in his role as Praepostor, witnessing punishment. His name is Patrick Wormald, and is the person with whom I later shared the editorship of the *Eton College Chronicle.*

I run the images again and again. I become fascinated by the over-maturity of these boys coupled with their total disconnection from what might appear to be normal life. Running around, rowing, strolling, gossiping, we could be participants in some outsize and exotic reality show. But the purpose of this Eton experiment is never clear to me. Why are we dressed in these strange clothes, like glamorous Hasids? What are all these barked orders in Latin? Playing the tape once more, I return to the main characters of my time at Eton. Here is Chummy talking less than convincingly about being modern. Here is Tony, my Trotskyist best friend and ally in subversion, from St. John's Wood. And here, glimpsed momentarily, out of focus and like a shadow over the proceedings, is the English Master, as elusive as ever. I still don't know what to think of him.

Briefly, I must explain my own botched rush into adulthood. Interest or ambition don't account for the fury with which at sixteen, I suddenly throw myself weekly into work. Indulgent Eton permits me to avoid most, but not all of the football or cricket field impositions. I know I want, more than anything, to do well. I want a scholarship at Oxford. There are mild burn-outs, but I am able to hide these successfully. Meanwhile, my father has grudgingly abandoned me to something he cannot any more control. I feel the force of his rage, which is expressed in relation to my intelligence as well as my own, no doubt tiresomely separate, life. Something has gone wrong for him, and it is myself. Only my mother knows what is going on, and doesn't disapprove. I am now surprised by my own ruthlessness. What I want, most of all, as boys often appear to do, is to rid myself of any vestige of innocence.

An early opportunity occurred in Paris, when I went to stay again with my grandmother. Here I smoked Gauloises, I cruised half-naked, uninterested girls with undone bikini strings, bad Parisian skin and lank Bardot hairdos at the stinking, floating swimming-pools which in those days lined the Seine. They wouldn't be interested in an Etonian. I made my Orangina last as I took another copious hit from *The Myth of Sisyphus.* 'The only serious philosophical question is suicide,' Albert Camus told me. I did manage to arrive at a resolution of sorts. I understood that what I had come to call 'the Eton thing' wouldn't last forever, and that it wasn't for me. Crossing the shimmery river to the Right Bank, I walked one day to the vicinity of the Halles. Many unattractive *filles de joie* clustered in those days around cheap hotels. I ascertained the rather modest cost of sexual experience by asking two of them, but lacked courage. Next day, however, I counted up the money I'd reserved for books. I walked back, circled the streets, and approached a 40-ish woman standing unromantically next to a kosher butcher's shop. (In those days, before the advent of boots and implants, and the importing of underage girls from Eastern Europe, Parisian streetwalkers still dressed smartly, wearing suits and blouses. I probably chose this one because she reminded me of a better-looking version of one of my well-to-do Protestant aunts.)

I can recall a stairway, a red counterpane in a small room with a frosted window that gives onto a dark, anonymous *cour*. The act itself was brief, unremarkable; but it seemed like experience of a sort. '*On dit que les anglais aiment les hommes*,' she tells me, pocketing notes, in what I perversely notice is grammatical French. '*Chez toi ce n'est évidemment pas le cas*.' Was this something she has been primed to say to every gangling, incompetent English boy? I didn't know whether to be pleased by the compliment, doubtful about its authenticity, or merely annoyed that she could see I was English.

One quite understandable error made when one is young is to believe in the power of a single transforming occurrence, be it politics, love or sex. Returning to Eton, I was struck by the degree to which my small adventure had changed nothing. I was as lonely as before, and I wanted more experience. How was I going to get it at Eton, of all places? I now hated even to hear about the round of crushes among boys. My visit in Paris (about which, I am not certain why, I determined to tell no-one) gave me fresh determination to avoid the sessions of mutual masturbation on offer. So I forced myself to look around. Perhaps there was something else I could learn here. Perhaps I hadn't been looking hard enough.

***

And I do begin to see that things are changing, after all. Suddenly, the reading of English classics seems exotic to me, even chic. The beak teaching English is a soft-voiced South African with cropped hair, and an intent, serious way of talking that is far from the overemphasis that characterises the efforts to communicate of Eton beaks. He tells us about irony, without apparently being able to apply it to himself. I suppose I learn that one can be serious about emotion, and that there is such a thing as sensibility. English seminars are conducted in rapt, hushed voices – his teaching of Shakespeare is known as the Agony Class. My own caustic, over-ironic Eton self doesn't know what to make of this. But perhaps there is something here that I need.

Meanwhile, through the often drearily detailed discussions of Hamlet's motivations in presenting himself as mad, or Lear's craziness, a startling development has occurred. Maybe I'm taunting, maybe there is something I understand about the English beak, which even he doesn't know. In relation to the many queeny, easily evaded beaks, he doesn't appear to be homosexual. I do understand that he's attracted to me, though I am not sure why, or what he wants. True to my own determination to change, however, I don't evade this interest. And I am surprised not to feel guilty.

In the meantime I find out about literature as rapidly as I can. The best time of my education is a class taught about Joseph Conrad's *The Heart Of Darkness* by the chain-smoking American literary critic, Lionel Trilling. He insists that I tell him about Kurtz's 'darkness' – what is it really, genuine illumination via a knowledge of human wickedness, or the ultimate lack of knowledge of the universe? Hating everything about chapel, I begin to worry myself into an acceptance of evil. Eton intimates to me that people aren't always good, just as it tells me that the past, no matter how hard we try, can never wholly be disposed of. Trilling and his wife Diana say that *Lolita* is the only good novel of the last years, though they quite like the first hundred pages of Norman Mailer's *The American Dream*. I buy both books, reading them with what I find to be genuine illumination.

I take the Trillings around Eton, watching them succumb to its charm. The literary critic asks me about the nieteenth century, how Eton compared with Rugby, and what Etonians actually learnt. Did they really learn nothing whatsoever? I haven't yet read his biography of Matthew Arnold, so I cannot know that he must regard Eton as the culmination of a genuine experiment in civilising gentlemen, mysteriously preserved. If I knew more, I could tell him that already, as far as I am concerned, I wish this experiment to fail, totally and comprehensively. Already I am mostly through with it. 'Style is so English a thing, and it may be a liability,' he tells me as we cross School Yard, shaking my hand. 'In England, style and intelligence can never be separated.'

'Yes,' I mutter, as I feel the force of this observation. For my part, I want to meet more people as wise and as urbane as Lionel Trilling. Rather than the violence displayed on television, this chain-smoking blazered Jewish intellectual becomes my image of contemporary 1960s America, and I resolve to go to New York as soon as I can.

***

But I realise that I must first accomplish an ancient Eton ritual, by undermining, not necessarily with fatal results, my own promise. In order truly to succeed, it now seems to me that I need to fail. I am amazed how deliberately I set out to do this and yet I now realize that this is a hallowed Eton way. In 1938, just before the Second World War broke out, when most thoughtful people were worrying about how to stand up to dictators, the literary critic Cyril Connolly wrote what remains the most interesting memoir of Eton, *Enemies of Promise*. Evoking what he calls the 'Theory of Permanent Adolescence', he describes a lifelong obsession with the circumstances of failure. What does it take to mess up one's gifts and inheritance so comprehensively that the fact of failure becomes a primary subject?

Connolly attributes his failure to Eton. He was supposed to succeed there, and he didn't. It's a bizarre theory, not least because Connolly is lacking in evidence when it comes to the facts of failure. He did, after all, succeed in the Eton arena, getting a scholarship to Oxford, editing the usual small magazine, and being elected to the Eton Society, wearing the coveted check trousers and silk waistcoat. He had the usual crushes (though these are the 1930s, and he displays a certain coyness when it comes to describing whether any sexual encounters actually took place.) Never quite daring to visit prostitutes in Paris, he remained a virgin. He suffered from a melancholy, attributable to adolescent miseries. His offence, described in deft but unconvincing detail, consisted in having used the Pop postal service (free, and one of the privileges of membership) to post letters from Collegers to their parents. In doing so he broke a rule, and allowed the richer Oppidan members of Pop to get sight of the lowly suburban addresses of the parents of Collegers:

> From that moment my vitality failed as I had seen it fail in others…I made the mistake, common in youth, of not understanding that people who like one for oneself, will overlook occasional lapses. I felt that the Members of the Eton Society liked me only in so far as I conformed while someone more mature would have known that the affair was trivial and that they liked me because I could never conform. Driven underground for a year by success, my persecution mania had found an outlet.

One might consider this small stuff indeed, even a bit ridiculous; but no, not at all. Connolly claims that he never fully recovered from the humiliation. Presumptuously, he wishes us to know that Eton failed him, as it did the entire British elite, because it turned him into a type, or a symbol. Swooningly, with many fine descriptions of the Thames valley, Connolly's book plays a clever variant on the middle-class theme of innocence betrayed and lost. Eton is both the magic place and the angel with the sword standing outside. It is where one goes to be ejected from the prospect of happiness. Nothing will ever be so good again.

**

Since its creation in 1863, the *Eton College Chronicle* has published accounts of the sporting, academic and cultural goings-on of the school. It is run by boys and, according to custom (though this is not always observed) the Master in charge doesn't censor the copy. Nowadays, the *Chronicle* is glossy, tabloidish, attention-seeking – the editors complain that there isn't enough money, but one wouldn't know this. In the context of Eton politics, however, the *Chronicle* is taken very seriously because, despite its minuscule circulation, it is read in newspaper offices and therefore becomes a conduit for good or bad publicity. Editors scrawl their unexpurgated accounts in a fat leather-bound book, and the comments are a fascinating mixture of graffiti and would-be erudition.

In 1975, for instance, one can learn that 'censorship took over… Oliver Letwin resigned his column, articles had to be shown to the censor before and after proofs.' In 1986 a joke ('RPCF – the name of a house – will be mounting attacks from behind') led to the carpeting of the editors. In 2003 the newspaper's censor was sacked for being in possession of Internet 'kiddie porn'. As one might expect, this was greeted with hilarity by the editors – a subsequent edition of the newspaper contained a fake ad for a catering firm bearing the sacked censor's name, and filled with ribald jokes.

One can examine red-bound copies of the *Chronicle* among Eton's more significant treasures, such as the Gutenberg Bible, in College Library, which is situated behind Lupton's Tower and within the Cloisters. The light yellow paper adorned with the Eton lilies, fleur-de lys and lion gives the publication an attractive retro style. In places the prose of contributors appears new-minted. I flip through a half-forgotten Marianne Faithfull concert ('her off-the-shoulder dress was much appreciated'), skim-read equally well-turned accounts of field games, a debate about the Vietnam War, avant-garde art exhibitions or European films. Fascinated, I observe how what goes on elsewhere comes filtered through these pages – it is interesting, for instance, to learn that after the 1965 election there were only three Labour M.P.s from Eton (there are two now) and 53 Conservatives, with one Ulster Unionist.

I am half-relieved to find that my own comments have been lost. But my co-editor's survive, and they depict, week by week, in exhaustive detail, our efforts to get round the censor and, as Patrick somewhat over-optimistically suggests, 'give a voice… to the undercurrent of Liberalism in the school.' Setting out to make waves, it is clear that Patrick and I succeeded only too well. For a brief moment, our leader articles were picked up regularly by the national press. 'We thought we could fire the press out,' Patrick comments, 'Well, it didn't work out that way.' Attacks on the curriculum, the system whereby boys are put down at birth, lead the Head Master to 'lose patience'. One issue (it contains what even now appears a slashing attack on the school by an anonymous Young Master; in reality, as I now recall, the English Master) leads to complaints from 25 per cent of the staff, and our effigies being burnt by a Library of disgusted Etonians.

Here is the issue devoted to the BBC's film when it was shown to a large audience on BBC1. Many people wonder whether this 'New Eton' we inhabit might not hold the keys to the future of British education. 'Would it not be possible for Britain to learn from Eton?' TV critics ask. Patrick and I beg to differ. And Patrick is complicated, tormented, an over-achiever on a scale that make my efforts seem minor. He sees Eton as 'a school with a personality, with customs modern, barbaric and eccentric… but of little more than average academic distinction.' Patrick has stayed up night after night, sweating over these words. Aged seventeen, he is quite the Thunderer. And now he expresses the view that Eton should become part of the state system.

At this stage, these are questions I cannot really answer –

because Eton still seems so unreal to me. 'You can take two views about Eton,' I start my own piece. 'Either it is one of the best institutions in the country (if not the best) or else it's an ugly wart on our egalitarian society.' Of course, it is both, I go on to say. In response to a BBC *Late Night Line-up* debate I strike what now appears to be a calculated note of adolescent weariness – though, I have to say, it still asks pertinent questions

Two facts came clearly out of the programme, First the Old Etonians were hardly like us... The second is that England is undoubtedly one of the most class-conscious countries in the world. Why should Etonians be 'sexually-maladjusted', why should they regard grammar school boys as complete aliens, why should they be out-moded Victorian relics? An hour of peak viewing time was devoted to solving or not solving these problems....

Week after week, we lay about ourselves – attacks on compulsory religion, assaults on the idea of school dress, the hierarchy of Pop and prefects. (The circulation doesn't rise, indeed it falls, as Patrick notes, due to 'alienation... from our persistently radical fare,') No matter – Patrick and I are totally happy with what we are doing. We back NGOs such as Amnesty – founded by an Etonian called Peter Benenson, and which we had introduced to the school some months previously. And, of course, we trash the Tories.

To summarise these weekly effusions, they are presumptuous without being exactly pompous. It is clear that we believe that we are stars in the making. But there is also a faintly Establishment tone about what we write, which gives our publication a comic air of schizophrenia – something which I later learn is shared by all public school revolutionaries. The word 'boredom' appears frequently in our weekly blasts. Much is boring about Eton, most of all its pretensions, notably 'the ponderous, deadening weight of the past'. Still, like good Etonians, we draw back from the most radical solutions. 'An Eton wholly modernised is unimaginable, even undesirable,' I find myself writing, 'just as an antiquated one is attractive but faintly ludicrous...' Did I really write something as pompous as this? Patrick's ultimate verdict on our efforts is touchingly, and quite unnecessarily, full of apologies: 'To my colleagues, particularly dear Nick, I say sorry for so much turbulence,' he concludes. 'I really am sorry.' Sorry for what, I ask so many years later. My own conclusion, I now realise, is somewhat different – I was happy for the first time, because I appeared to have broken the rules without being punished. This is the best thing I did when I was young.

The author – leaver's photo, 1964

***

Like so many before me, I did experience the rush upstairs of boys in check trousers signalling my election to Pop. It would be foolish to deny that I was happy as a consequence; though I still dreamed about rooms in Paris with red counterpanes and leggy occupants. I loved my green or red Chinese motif silk waistcoats more than I can say, and wearing check trousers with boots that I did for once in my life keep clean. I loved the way people would smile at me in the street now. And I loved the way girls would always come and see me, though in the crucial matter of popped or un-popped bras there was little change. But these good things weren't in the end enough. I had got up too much, pushed myself too hard, and now (in my heart of hearts, I knew this) I must pay for it. So I staged my own form of revolt – by smoking and swallowing never very interesting pills. As a member of Pop I could get permission to go to London for the theatre. I didn't always attend these plays, going clubbing instead. There was another visit to a prostitute, this time in the bedsit wilds of Pimlico. (Without the French overlay of *sagesse,* or the bidet, I found the experience rather less illuminating; and it caused me to wonder whether one couldn't lose innocence without gaining any experience.)

Now, I asked myself, what I should do about the English Master. He was sending him affectionate notes at this time, and promised, through the medium of literature to be sure, and prudently, real life, even passion. Moral thoughts were what he offered, good ideas about how to live honestly; and to that end he gave me such writers as D.H. Lawrence. Even in my self-absorbed state I could tell that he had fallen in love with me. In his room, where I gave a heavily edited account of my hidden life, I did once suggest consummation within Eton, wherever he cared. Though I didn't say so, my point was that I didn't care one way or another. I wanted merely to hurry up, and be grown up. But I sensed even then that I wasn't being wholly honest. Homosexuality, perpetrated with minors or adults, was still a criminal offence. No-one as cautious as he was would be willing to take such a risk. I began a confessional novel of adolescence, of which (references to masturbation and hookers excised) I published an excerpt in the *Chronicle*.

One night, returning late from another non-theatrical London visit, I got myself caught. Within the Eton consttution (as I well understood) an offence committed by a member of Pop could be dealt with only by the Head Master. In previous times such a chastisement would have been meted out in the presence of a member of Pop and another from the Sixth Form (rendering the punishment of Pop rare, if not quite unthinkable). Chummy had changed all this by his habit of private chastisement. I didn't believe that I would be beaten – because the offence wasn't serious enough. I would probably get away with it, as I had done so far. Or so I thought as I made my way across School Yard the following evening to Chummy's lodgings.

I went through the Cloister, climbing the stairs and pushing at a green baize door. Here I was brought short by a sharp whiff of danger – as soon as I saw Chummy's expression I knew that I had miscalculated. There were large chintz chairs and sofas, and I looked around me for instruments of torture. Chummy was dressed in ecclesiastical garb, a thick, light brown belt around his small pot belly. The first thing I noticed was a strong odour of alcohol on his breath. He seemed very small when we came momentarily to be standing together. As I stood before one of the ample, chintz-covered sofas, he embarked on what proved to be a long monologue. I was one of the boys in whom he had vested most hopes for the future. And I had let him down, giving him no alternative but to punish me. At this moment he paused, seeming to look for a half-filled glass that wasn't there. He told me that this was nothing to do with my editorship of the newspaper. 'We do welcome controversy,' he said. 'It keeps us modern, doesn't it?' I do not recall whether I responded to this piece of hypocrisy.

Sniffing, Chummy came to the point. Either I would be expelled from the school forthwith, despite the fact that only four weeks remained of what was my last term, or I must submit to being beaten by him. I didn't really think I should waste time considering these options. Trying to retain some semblance of Eton poise as I positioned myself over a wing of a sofa, I was nonetheless astonished when Chummy, after undoing my belt, pulled down first my check trousers, and my underpants. I could hear heavyish breathing, finally the sound of a glass emptied and replaced on the table. Then he began to smack my naked bum with his hand, not so that it hurt him or myself in any way, but slowly enough for me to be aware of the fact that he was weeping profusely. Again I noticed how strong his breath smelt of whisky. After he had finished (there were, I believe, ten smacks, or pats) and I had pulled up my underpants and trousers, he began to say how sorry he was to have hurt me, and how much he loved me. He said that he had loved all those whom he had hurt in his life. I think I heard him say how much he hated himself. Then he turned his back on me, motioning me to leave.

I told few people about this experience, and to those with whom I did share the secret I gave a sharply edited version. This was out of shame, but also because I really didn't understand what had happened. I felt humiliated, and I was damaged more than I could ever have brought myself to express. I had brought this downfall on myself. What was he doing with me? This is why I thought it best if I, too, kept quiet. And who would have believed me anyhow? So I served out my remaining time at Eton. I did catch Chummy's bloodshot eye once or twice, but he appeared to avoid me. When I came before him to collect a leaving book, by tradition the *Poems of Thomas Gray*, he appeared not to recognize me. In School Yard, I looked at the *Ode on a Distant Prospect of Eton College,* a poem which, of course, I hated:

> Alas! Regardless of their doom,
> The little victims play!
> No sense have they of ills to come,
> Nor care beyond today..

There was indeed nothing more for me to say. On my last day, I packed hurriedly, in anticipation of release. But I could tell as I did so, waiting for my mother, that this wasn't the end of the story. I would have many years in which to contemplate what happened to me at Eton, and what I became.

CHAPTER SIX

The earliest leaving pictures appear to have been given by rich boys to the Head Master, along with a parting gift of money. More than 200 of these exist – rows and rows of young aristocrats, exhibited side by side in a wood panelled room, who appear to look down at the spectator from the uplands of privilege. A first glance makes one gasp at the collective effrontery. ('They're so beautiful, and so cruel,' a left-wing American professor once said to me.) On closer examination these Etonians prove, as one might expect, to be a fascinating combination of the highly successful, the averagely so, and the utterly obscure. Here's Sir William Young, author of travel books and Governor-to-be of Tobago, and here, book in hand, is Richard Wellesley, elder brother of the military genius, the

Duke of Wellington, about to modernise India. The dark-browed, melancholic, already portly figure of Charles James Fox, reckless gambler and equally reckless aristocratic dissident, shares pride of place with his nephew, who spent time in France, returning in order to sponsor a radical chic salon, here portrayed in a red, sans-culottish Pop-style waistcoat, hand held, Napoleon-style, to his breast. Here are Hallam, *père et fils*, respectively the author of a best-selling Whig work on constitutional government, and the much lamented friend of Tennyson, and inspiration for *In Memoriam:*

Dear as the mother to the son,
More than my brothers are to me.

Many didn't amount to very much at all – the diminutive William Damer, for instance, who 'passed his life with troops of women and the blind fiddler', marrying a sculptress, bankrupting his estate and killing himself, aged 32, in a Covent Garden brothel; and the chubby-cheeked William Legge, 4th Earl of Darmouth, who, in the style of a Hilaire Belloc character, voted against the 1832 Reform Bill long after his fellow-peers had abandoned the field of privilege.

Here they sit as Etonians, unchangeable, in some transcendent state of glamour and equality. The same lustre adheres to the near-numberless rows of leaving photographs given in modern times. From Chas, Will, Don, Hal, they say – or simply, To Nick (use of the first name in a dedication is a sign of social favour – omission meant that one didn't really know the recipient, who was sent the photograph for form's sake). On the fly leaf are recollections of obscure moments of friendship – perhaps rivalry in love will be coyly expressed, in relation to either sex. Over the centuries these Etonians gaze out towards their friends in the frozen state of early adulthood. Who or what could divert such figures from their chosen paths?

Etonians do marry each other's sisters, do do the same sort of jobs, do further each other's careers. At moments in their lives they are mysteriously available for each other. But the idea of a Masonic Etonness is a relatively recent occurrence in the school's history. Self-consciousness about the role of the school, and a desire to acknowledge its power, appears to have begun with the patronage of Queen Victoria. From 1860, books extolling the superior qualities of Eton were published in substantial numbers. An early proponent of the Eton cult was George Nathaniel Curzon, a quintessential OE. At Eton, where he was Captain of the Oppidans, Curzon displayed precocious administrative zeal by putting a stop to nude bathing. (He reorganised the Fourth of June festival, giving it most of its modern features, buying champagne further afield than the traditional

Windsor supplier, and rationing it, in order to minimise drunkenness; and the *Daily News* reported that his speech was 'as melodious, as clear and as flexible as it is possible to conceive.') Curzon was more than loath to discard the glories of school, describing election to Pop as 'the best day of my life'. Acquaintances predicted that Oxford would be for him merely 'that brief interval which must intervene between Eton and the cabinet.' Famous lines were composed about him by two Balliol contemporaries:

My name is George Nathaniel Curzon,
I am a most superior person,
My cheek is pink, my hair is sleek,
I dine at Blenheim once a week.

Curzon became something of a caricature of himself, though it is not clear whether he objected to this. (He is said to have remarked, on glimpsing soldiers bathing on the Western Front, 'Dear me, I had no idea the lower classes had such white skins.') A great restorer of homes, a great giver of poorly extemporised orations, Curzon kept up his ties with Eton. As Viceroy of India, he presided over the annual Old Etonian dinner in Simla, summer residence of the Raj; and in England he returned to the school year after year, in order to address the boys, for whom, as Foreign Secretary, he kept the doors of advancement open. When Curzon jestingly suggested at another Fourth of June speech that the school's recent record should give it the right to appoint Viceroys in perpetuity, the suggestion was taken seriously by Indian newspapers, leading to a torrent of outraged letters and editorials. Curzon's early experience with pageants at Eton bequeathed a lasting fascination with processions. He staged the magnificent durbar, celebrating the Coronation of Edward VII with Anglo-Indian magnificence. Late in his career, in 1920, he organised the postwar Remembrance Day after the First World War, which is still commemorated according to his rules.

Etonmania went naturally with the chummy arrangements based on dynastic preference that characterised British politics in the late-imperial age. There were always enough adequately connected Etonians to form a government, and not all of them were stupid. A.J. Balfour was an Old Etonian, and in his well-born, clubbable cabinet of 1902 as many as half were appointed as a consequence of what David Gilmour, Curzon's biographer, calls 'the hierarchical mysteries of Etonian ritual' – cousins, cousins' husbands, etc. (Lord Lansdowne, who had been the Prime Minister's fagmaster at Eton, remained at the Foreign Office, while Londonderry, who had been the Prime Minister's fag, was promoted to the Board of Education.)

Gossip, 1937

How much influence did Etonians ever really wield on each others' behalf? In 1965 the liberal author Anthony Sampson (educated at the more meritocratic and middle-class Westminster) concluded that their influence had been considerable, and should be diminished. He believed that the real Etonian crime was excessive confidence. In Sampson's best-selling *Anatomy of Britain*, Etonians controlled such commanding heights as the Court, City boardrooms, the army (though this didn't seem to matter so much in the 1960s) and, above all, the Tory party. The wisdom of having Etonians dominate Tory politics, Sampson suggested, was most brutally pointed up in a famous 1963 *Spectator* article by the liberal Tory Ian Macleod, which gave a detailed account of the goings-on of the 'magic circle' of Etonians who had handed the succession from Harold Macmillan to Alec Douglas-Home. Naming the conspirators, Macleod asserted, correctly, that eight of the nine went to Eton. Macleod was outraged that Douglas-Home appointed 11 Etonians to his own cabinet. No place could be found for himself.

So much jobbery combined with the Old School tie sat uneasily with the egalitarianism of the 1960s, and Sampson was much influenced by Macleod's observations. He believed that Etonians should now, in an act of supremely good breeding, step aside so that 'the ablest boys' (i.e. those from grammar schools, though Sampson perhaps also meant his own school, too) could display 'social confidence in themselves'. When I met Sampson shortly before he died, he said that he might have exaggerated the evil influence of Etonians. 'It was fashionable to bash Eton in the 1960s – and I rather feel that I contributed to a myth of Eton supremacy,' he said. 'But I still feel that it is remarkable how good Etonians are at politics. I'd meet them everywhere I went. Even in post-colonial Africa, on the side of the angels, Etonians were to be found – and I've never understood why they were so good at networking and politics.'

Etonians did dominate public life in Britain in the 1950s and early 1960s, and this probably had to do with the post-war exhaustion and stuffiness of the time as well as the many years of Tory government. There was indeed much that was cloying, philistine and complacent about Macmillan, with his empty slogan 'You've never had it so good.' Prosperity appeared to coexist, in the short term at least, with reinforced class divisions. The most lasting legacy of the Macmillan era was environmental – and profoundly negative – ugly housing, including tower blocks and the spoilation of the countryside. However, not every member of this Eton public class proved to be influential or indeed powerful. (Geoffrey Wheatcroft tells the story of Sir Walter Bromley-Davenport, 'a Grenadier, a boxing enthusiast, all in all a Tory of the Old School' who, as a Party Whip, mistook the Belgian ambassador for a recalcitrant Tory MP, kicking him downstairs – and there must have been many Sir Walters.) As conspiracy, ultimately, the Eton connection rates somewhere near the myth of the Cliveden set, according to which appeasement was arranged in the Astor family sitting-room – it is good to hear, but not wholly convincing.

'There was a glut of Old Etonians in public life in the early 1960s,' Jonathan Aitken recalls. 'It was at this time that the journalist Henry Fairlie invented the phrase "the

Establishment" And the *Queen* magazine, no less, ran an article in which the heads of all the boys in an Eton house photograph were replaced by contemporary Estabishmentarians – the Chairman of Barings, etc.' But Aitken recalls that the moment of Etonian supremacy was of brief duration. The Labour Party had no time for Eton toffs (though more austere Wykehamists were tolerated). 'After the Macmillan era there were jobs that just didn't go to Etonians. There was a joke to the effect that outside the school gates was hung a sign: "Cabinet-makers to the Queen."'

***

Eton influence was substantial, of course; but it was also fitful and, as one might imagine, most effective when grafted onto other British institutions frequented by Etonians. In particular, the link between Eton and the Brigade of Guards appears to have been significant. Guardsmen Etonians were most influential in the Tory party, providing its twentieth-century grandees. Harold Macmillan, Oliver Lyttelton, 'Bobbety' Cranborne and Harry Crookshank were at Eton together. (Nouveaux-riches Crookshank and Macmillan were scholars; Lyttelton and Cranborne, the one a son of an Eton head master, the

155

other from the aristocratic Cecil family, were Oppidans). Both Crookshank and Macmillan, were buried alive and nearly killed in neighbouring patches of mud in Flanders. Crookshank was castrated, wearing a surgical truss for the rest of his life. It took Macmillan 25 years, another war and another near-fatal war experience – this time an escape from being burnt alive in a plane crash – before he acquired the imperturbability and ruthlessness for which he became famous as Prime Minister. Like Curzon, these Guardsman Etonians kept in touch with the school, and they alluded to its influence in their diaries. When not dressing up in dinner jackets for dinner, or tweeds for slaughtering grouse, they dutifully wore their dark-and-light blue ties.

Are Etonians Nature's Wets (a perception which reached prominence in the Thatcher era, when, as an old man, Harold Macmillan was to be heard urging Mrs. Thatcher not to 'sell the family silver' by disposing of nationalised assets, and indeed bemoaning her assault on the union power of the miners, 'our boys', as he called them)? Aitken believes so. 'Etonians who are politicians have always felt that they inhabit the Big House,' he says. 'The little people mustn't be thrown out into the streets. One can always find the odd tied cottage behind the stables for their old age. That's the Eton mentality applied to politics, and it does tend to make them Wets, or One Nation people, or whatever phrase you care to use.'

Among twentieth-century Etonian Tories, however, significant differences of opinion are to be found. The Guardsmen, perhaps because they had (most of them, at least) nearly lost their lives in defence of their country, opposed Hitler from the beginning. So did Anthony Eden. Others, notably the egregious Londonderry, were admirers of the dictators, courting them assiduously. This appears to have been the consequence of delusions about British power rather than an attraction to fascism. The appeaser Lord Halifax (who fagged for Londonderry) is well-described by the American historian John Lukacs:

His appearance was unusual: very tall, very gaunt and erect, he had a stance marked by his unusually large, splayed feet; he was born without a left hand, the prosthetic substitution for which (a fist) he managed exquisitely, as indeed he wore his unobtrusive but exquisitely cut clothes. His aristocratic appearance accorded well with his character: calm and cool, perhaps even cold; shy rather than sensitive; always in control of his emotions, and perhaps more admirably, of his ambitions. He had a faint (rather than weak) sense of humour... His main interests – indeed addictions –were fox-hunting, High Anglicanism, and high government service..

Etonian politicians, and Harold Macmillan most of all, were happy to be identified as believers in some variety of a nation-state capable of protecting all British citizens, rich and poor, and this can be laid to a patrician Eton tradition of *noblesse oblige*. They practised the art of back-stabbing, sometimes on each other, though this is an activity not confined to Etonians. Outside social connections it is hard to say what tied together these Etonians other than the enjoyment of wearing out their trousers sitting around tables with their old school friends, and the notion, above all, that power was theirs to exercise while their wealth allowed them to indulge in the call of public duty.

Ten, mostly vintage Etonians served in Harold Macmillan's 1957 cabinet. Macmillan's tweeded, bewhiskered appearance was astutely contrived. As the historian Tony Judt observes, he was 'a middle-class trimmer masquerading as an Edwardian country gentleman.' Selling withdrawal abroad and prosperity at home, he was an appropriate leader for the time. His successor, who abandoned his peerage to become Prime Minister (legalisation was passed to make this possible, transforming him from Lord Home to Sir Alec Douglas-Home) was distinctly less suitable for the job. At Eton, Sir Alec had been known as, simply, Alec Dunglass, and this is how Cyril Connolly enviously described him:

He was a votary of the esoteric Eton religion, the kind of graceful, tolerant, sleepy boy who is showered with favours, and crowned with all the laurels, who is liked by the masters and admired by the boys without any apparent exertion on his part, without experiencing the ill-effects of success himself or arousing the pangs of envy in others. In the eighteenth century he would have become Prime Minister before he was thirty; as it was he appeared honourably ineligible for the struggle of life.

Sir Alec made the mistake of resorting to his pipe and matchbox when explaining his economics policy on the relatively new medium of television. Pitted against Harold Wilson, a worldly Oxford economist (and grammar school boy), he had no chance whatsoever. Nowadays, Sir Alec is remembered as the perfect butt for a generation of satirists, who cruelly captured his never-grown-up, young-old-man languorous, Edwardian style.

In Ted Heath and Margaret Thatcher, the Tories discovered strains of non-patrician radicalism. Etonians continued to occupy cabinet posts (posh ones indeed) but they didn't dominate Toryism. There were a number of grandees in Mrs. Thatcher's first cabinet ('Wets' like Sir Ian Gilmour, grandees like Lord Soames and Lord Carrington) but they were spectacularly expelled in 1983. As Geoffrey Wheatcroft shows in *The Strange Death of Tory England,* Mrs. Thatcher finished off the old Tory elite of Etonians in what appears to have been an act of class vengeance. They could certainly never be taken seriously again. Why had anyone ever believed in their mystique? Part of the fascination of Alan Clark's 1970s and 1980s diaries lies in the fact that their Etonian author knows he is wholly absurd. All the Eton slang ('mobbed' meaning harassed, as one does a bad teacher; the omnipresent non-correct 'spastic', for hopeless; expressions from the Field Game like 'heads down, bully and shove'), all the ostentatious talking up of his admiration for 'The Lady' cannot conceal from Clark the knowledge that he is finished, whatever he does.

How can a toff survive in an ostensibly meritocratic milieu? How does one avoid being thought a fool? Many stratagems can be adopted, and one of them is to do as Clark does – play up to expectations, be outrageous. Appear more drunk in public than you really are, slurring in the House. Don't disavow remarks about black politicians being sent back to 'Bongo Bongo Land'. Praise Hitler if it gets you noticed. If people think of you as dissolute, oblige them by making passes at strangers on trains while carrying red ministerial boxes. No-one outdoes Clark when it comes to grovelling, but the dullards (and they include many of the 'wet' or merely dim Etonians to be found clogging the House) do it far worse, and with no style – they are true members of the OBN (Order of the Brown Nose). Part-club, part-Eton, the House of Commons is a disappointing place. Everyone fails, and disgrace is never far away. But, unless sacked (not an infrequent occurrence, and something only just avoided by Clark) no-one ever wholly leaves a school of which Margaret Thatcher is the ferocious Dame. And this is how the Eton thing ends, shining, endlessly present, like the rotting wood in Clark's castle. Spite furnishes the best way to go. And then, infrequently, the past returns, as in this description of Harold Macmillan's memorial service in Westminster Abbey:

The Grenadiers' Return was played, and I thought of the fife music and the decimated battalion marching back from Hulluch on 26 September 1915, past the wounded, laid out in rows... groaning from their injuries. And the young classical scholar, less than a year out of Eton, pale and shaken but heroic nonetheless. When Macmillan enlisted, Britain was at the very height of her power and dominion. The habitual bearing, stoicism, self-sacrifice, sense of 'fair play': the whole *tenue* of the English upper class was in place and unquestioned, looked up to and copied everywhere.

Now look at us – and them!

***

Just as Eton accommodated grandees and swots, the rich and the less rich, so, too, it proved to be a home of sorts to Rebels as well as Hons. There were always *other* Old Etonians, not so many of them perhaps, who held somewhat different views to those of the Tory majority. One can examine books about the school, and see how, from the 1920s onwards, a strain of criticism begins to emerge amid so much celebration. Homosexuality is a theme of *Decent Fellows,* a novel published in 1930 to the disgust of parents. (Its author, John Heygate, son of a House Master, was a producer at the BBC; but he is mostly remembered for having run off with Evelyn Waugh's first wife.) It is possible, though not entirely convincing, to see the disastrous career of the homosexual spy Guy Burgess (also a BBC producer, among many other carefully contrived front activities of which the most effective was, of course, being an Etonian) as an act of revolt against Eton. ('Boys are cheap today/ Cheaper than yesterday,' was how he entertained camp friends in Tangier, to the strains of the 'Boating Song', long before he was sent by MI6 to Washington, a posting as catastrophic as it remains hard to explain.) Donald Maclean, also a spy, was an Etonian; and so, too, was the fellow-traveller John Strachey, later a Labour minister, and responsible for the notorious policy of purchasing most of the world's harvest of snoek, a fish that even famished post-war British families refused to eat.

The question of whether George Orwell was or was not a typical Etonian, or even a recognisable one, is aired in most of his biographies. The gangly, monosyllabic Eric Blair succeeded in assuming a protective coloration of obscurity at Eton. After four and a half years, he left school in 1921, bottom of his election in his final exams, and 117th out of the 140 boys of his year. A Colleger, 'a bit of a Bolshie', Eric Blair appears to have steadily raised the failure stakes at Eton. He did play the Wall Game, helping to score one of the only goals in the history of the sport – a rare moment of achieved prominence against all odds that is wholly Winston Smith. Orwell formed a lasting distaste for the 'pansy' aesthetes who edited Eton's poetry magazines, and there are those who suggest that he dabbled in paranormal vengeance by making soap effigies out of his enemies, though no indication of their success is recorded. As a member of the Sixth Form he even acquired a 'fag', though Anthony Wagner (later to occupy the post of Garter Knight at Arms) admitted that 'he did not talk much.' Much of the time he remained invisible, and thus inviolate. The best one can say is that at Eton Eric Blair was left alone to become himself.

First a Burmese colonial policeman, then a *plongeur* in a Paris restaurant, finally a vagrant, Orwell rejected his old school, along with most of the England that had made him. In the 1930s, he referred to his 'five years in a lukewarm bath of snobbery' at Eton while trashing friend Cyril Connolly's book for its self-indulgence. (When Connolly suggested that public school experiences were 'so intense as to dominate their lives and to arrest their development', Orwell observed: 'Your first impulse is to look for the misprint. Presumably there is a "not" left out or something. But no, not a bit of it.') He remained scathing about Eton. 'I did no work there and learned very little,' he informed readers of a left-wing American magazine. Much to the irritation of his Eton ex-friends, he said that he had been unhappy at school because his family were poor. 'I don't feel that Eton has been much of a formative influence in my life,' he suggested. In response to the observation attributed to Wellington about the playing fields of Eton, Orwell replied that the first battles of succeeding wars were lost there.

Never appearing, or indeed wishing to be a literary genius, displaying a modesty quite at odds with the scale of his achievement, Orwell remains so great a writer because of his dogged, passionate self-application in relation to the pursuit of truthfulness. He is able to discard unnecessary baggage – not just the upper-class stuff, or the Southwold tea-room milieu of his family, but also the progressive stupidities of his time. Long after the less persistent have quit the field, Orwell is willing, stubbornly, immovably, to stay around, nagging, exhorting or simply telling us how things are. It's easy to see why he would have hated to be thought to owe anything to Eton. But one can surely acknowledge Orwell's 'one of a kind', bizarrely constructed identity while making allowance for a few, never wholly eradicated Eton traits. He does remain, in the shabby clothes and with his assumed proletarian manner, some sort of recognisable Etonian figure. Would he really have bothered to subject himself to so much accumulated misery if he hadn't wanted to eradicate every vestige of what he deemed to be class privilege? It isn't fanciful to see in his often brutally simple language an assault conducted on the classical education which he despised for its fake, over-rhetorical fluency and its un-English pretentiousness – and which, in true Orwell style, he claimed, unconvincingly to be sure, to have forgotten.

In *Homage to Catalonia,* Orwell tells us that he sang the 'Boating Song' in the Spanish trenches near Huesca, shortly before his vocal chords were irretrievably damaged by a bullet. One of the waiters in *Down and Out in Paris and*

London is described as looking like an Eton boy. Orwell returned to some of his Eton acquaintances as he became successful. He corresponded with masters, re-befriending both Cyril Connolly and the novelist Anthony Powell. Orwell's two greatest patrons were the left-wing baronet-publisher Richard Rees (a possible model for Ravelstoke in *Keep the Aspidistra Flying*) and the editor of the *Observer,* David Astor, both Etonians. It was Astor who fixed him up with the house in Jura where he wrote *1984* (the island belonged to an Etonian friend of Astor's), later arranging his deathbed marriage and his burial in a Buckinghamshire churchyard. When Astor asked him whether he would ever consider sending his son to Eton, Orwell complained only of the dress code, which 'made a fool of a boy'. (Orwell, about whom Connolly said that 'he couldn't blow his nose without moralising about conditions in the handkerchief industry,' might rather have wanted Etonians to sport a version of the dyed black A.R.P. battledress that he was so proud to wear when off-duty during the blitz.)

It appears that Orwell reclaimed at least some of his earlier identity as be became older and sicker, and many witnesses describe a recognisable public school manner beneath the faux-proletarian drawl. When his Etonian landlord paid a visit to the small Jura cottage in which he was writing, he sent another, less posh visitor into the kitchen. He appeared nostalgic towards the past of privilege even as he insisted that its day had gone. His last review for the *Observer*, dictated in 1948 as he lay dying in hospital, is of a book entitled *Eton Medley*. It contains the usual criticisms of irrelevance and privilege. The top hats and tail coats, Orwell notes, 'had charm and function so long as they represented the kind of elegance that everyone looked up to,' but in a 'shabby and democratic country', they are no more than a nuisance. Most striking is Orwell's unexpected praise for Eton:

It has one great virtue... and that is a tolerant and civilised atmosphere which gives each boy a chance of developing his own individuality. The reason is perhaps that, being a very rich school, it can afford a large staff, which means that masters are not overworked; and also that Eton partly escaped the reforms set on foot by Dr. Arnold and retained certain characteristics belonging to the eighteenth century and even to the Middle Ages. At any rate, whatever its future history, some of its traditions deserve to be remembered.

No school could ask for a more fulsome tribute from its most prominent rebel.

Something of the Eton cult survives in the regular dinners given in commemoration of House Masters by their Old Boys, and held in a large room known as the Election Chamber, in the red-brick, crenellated sixteenth-century Lupton's Tower. After the 40-odd, dinner-jacketed, mostly brick-complexioned, often stoutish Old Boys have sat down, the proceedings begin. The Provost makes a speech asking for money, and a tribute is paid to the House Master (in this instance the heartily disliked disciplinarian who passed me on to Chummy for punishment) who also speaks, fondly recalling the past. Tribute is stiffly paid to him by one or more of his favourite boys. After the grim food has been eaten, and the port passed round, there is a chance to work out what became of all those smiling leaving photo figures. Have they descended into the safe mire of middle age? Do they have sons at Eton – or have their offspring not been accepted, due to the school's rising academic standards? Do they recall each other's sporting exploits – and did they ever meet each other's wives?

Now choice pieces of business gossip can be discreetly passed on. One may exchange addresses while catching up on hunting accidents. In the background, however, hovers something less utilitarian – though one might hesitate to call it spiritual. Those who have been successful (those who have not been, in my experience, rarely attend such meetings) can reminisce about a past that is now safely filed away. There is no boasting – that would be poor form indeed. The notion that one has fulfilled at least something of early promise is enough to connect the past with the happily uneventful present.

On such doubtful propositions, and with many such scenes, is constructed a book with the best claim to describe what it means to believe in the Eton past. This is Anthony Powell's *A Dance to the Music of Time,* a twelve-volume cycle of novels written over a period of twenty years, from the 1950s to the 1970s. The action begins with three boys messing together in late 1920s Eton. Through the window we see a solitary figure run through drizzle – 'hobbling unevenly, though with determination, on the flat heels of running shoes.' This is Widmerpool, butt of jokes, social climber, a figure of insuperable self-regard matched only by the desire for humiliation. Talk turns from the quality of sausages to the more important matter of Widmerpool's overcoat:

At this distance of time, I cannot remember precisely what sort of an overcoat Widmerpool was said to have worn in the first instance. Stories about it have grown into legend; so much so that even five or six years after you might still occasionally hear an obtrusive or inappropriate garment referred to as 'a Widmerpool'; and Templer, for example, would sometimes say: 'I am afraid I am wearing rather Widmerpool socks today,' or 'I've bought a wonderful Widmerpool tie to go home in'. My impression is that the overcoat's initial deviation from normal was slight, depending on the existence or absence of a belt at the back, the fact that the cut was single- or double-breasted...

Powell tells us that that the overcoat is remarkable only 'for the comment it aroused', and this is true of his work, which is concerned with the circumstances in which the same or similar narratives, decade after decade, can be told and retold, without interest being exhausted. He makes much of the passing of time, prefacing each 'season' of the cycle with allusions to high art and mortality; but his real subject is the life and death of information, or, put more crudely, gossip. People die in Powell's work; but with only one or two exceptions, this happens as a matter of course. It is the way one appears to others that matters, the way one carries off things, or evades them; and not the awful, truly significant matters of life.

Powell's narrator Nick appears immured in his own past

and his tightly tailored cult of social scruple. It would be nice to think that this is Powell's devious way of wondering aloud about the cost of parasitical snobbery, but one can never be sure. The same is true of the lavishly described world inhabited by Powell's characters. Boredom oozes through each excessively nuanced description; but some sort of line drawn around every scene forbids its acknowledgement by the author. Powell could never have managed the poignant end of Evelyn Waugh's war trilogy, in which the snobbish, anti-Semitic, arch-Catholic Guy Crouchback finally cracks under pressure, acquiring a measure of defeated humanity in relation to his own inability to save a group of Jews, who have somehow escaped gassing, from being despatched to the Stalinist Gulag. Powell is far too wary and controlled for such unruly emotions; after so many volumes, the reader may wish to conclude that, in common with his subjects, he doesn't understand them.

Widmerpool (no-one would dream of calling him by his ghastly first name, Kenneth) is what Etonians call a 'total crasher' – a person whom lack of looks, style, family origins (and, though the snobbish Powell doesn't stress this, money) debar from serious consideration. He passes from Eton into the City, through the Army and into fellow-travelling left-wing politics, thence into the progressive academe of the 1960s, rising as a consequence of the same hopelessly applied effort that distinguished his thrice-weekly runs. Powell is generous with his disapprobation, presenting Widmerpool both as voyeur and masochist. In an early, brilliant delineation of political correctness, the awful Kenneth represents the fads and failings of each decade. But the real purpose of these volumes is a restitution of sorts. Widmerpool, observed by narrator Nick, must be punished for his presumptuous dullness – wherever possible, he must be paid in kind. In Volume Two a girl pours a receptacle filled with sugar over Widmerpool's head at a dreary deb dance, thus enlivening the proceedings. This is a good joke, and everybody laughs.

Many, many years, and some good jokes later, Widmerpool marries a woman who turns out to be both frigid and insatiable. (Powell's women, in line with the fantasies of his time, are vamps or doormats; sex often appears to take place, as was said about Anthony Eden, in double-breasted pyjamas.) There are more jokes to come – when, for instance, the hapless Widmerpool arranges for his wife to couple with an ageing French Stalinist only to witness the latter die, purple-faced, of his vain exertions. Pamela slips further into her own darkness, causing the death of an infatuated writer, and finally encompassing her own death (i.e. not quite being around to witness her own, ultimate non-enjoyment of a final sexual act) in the arms of an

American academic, and in the less than salubrious circumstances of a Paddington hotel. Meanwhile, Widmerpool finishes his career as a member of a sect he has encountered through his stewardship of a 'new' university – Powell's contempt for the levelling aspect of the 1960s is quite explicit – wearing blue robes, and running again, this time without any clothes and by night, in search of religious fulfilment. Final humiliation occurs at a posh wedding given in a country house by an acquaintance of his and Nick's (also an Old Etonian) just before his death from over-exertion. Widmerpool abases himself on all fours, causing guests to trip over him as he cravenly begs forgiveness for his own awfulness. No-one is very interested, and he dies as he has lived, a crasher and a disgrace to the school.

In the hands of a writer less talented and less snobbish – someone not wholly fascinated by the purposelessly rotating wheels of social ritual – Widmerpool might seem poignant. His ineptitude could be a means of reflecting on the mediocre scene in which he rises, or a platitudinous comment, perhaps, on the way in which industry can be made to overcome lack of native gifts. But Powell truly dislikes his own creation, and it is the rough surfaces in the books, not the somewhat vapid set-pieces about culture, art, mortality etc., that make them absorbing. What is it about Widmerpool that makes Powell hate him so much? The answer is to be found back at Eton, with the offending over-coat. Good form is how people survive in the face of persistent disappointment; and for Powell, style is the way one should marshal experience. One must realise who or what just won't do. Also, style is the only true criterion of success – something that the style-proof Widmerpool, consumed by ambition, fails to realise. Powell's great achievement is to have transposed this somewhat remote Eton notion of what is fitting, and what is not, onto the society of his time, at the moment when it was vanishing. This is the true, though perhaps not lasting, significance of his work.

Powell-worship has diminished somewhat since his death in 2000, but there are still trainspotter types who club together (sometimes even meeting at Eton) in order to decide whether X or Y is the model for his characters. Lord Longford, Powell's brother-in-law, took a personal interest in this controversy. Perhaps because he was a jogger, venturing forth on country lanes each day in a yellow pullover and jodhpurs when he wasn't swimming in the nude, many newspaper columnists suggested that he might be Widmerpool. I was surprised by this – because Longford, although he was extremely vain, displayed a flamboyance, and a genuine eccentricity, as well as a periodic kindness, not evident in the dourly self-absorbed Widmerpool. When I asked him what he thought of this, Longford giggled happily. He didn't think that he was Widmerpool (he might have said that this would have implied an act of sadism on the part of his sister's husband), but he might well be 'a bit of Erridge'. When I pointed out that he couldn't very well be seen as the somewhat saintly, reclusive Orwell-like peer who espouses left-wing causes, living in squalid seclusion with an ex-model, Longford smiled indulgently, as if in possession of a secret he didn't wish to disclose. 'Tony was very careful when he cast his characters,' he said.

***

On St. Jermyn's street, or in the paved arcades around it, shops still sell O.E. Eton Viking or Eton Rambler ties, Eton cufflinks, along with grey or blue old-fashioned double-breasted suits, funny checked shirts, dark and light blue suspenders or braces, and the sort of soft, ill-fitting hat once worn to the races with a rakish tilt, known as a 'titfer'. I halt, examining the exhibits with amazement. I have never dressed like this, and I wonder who does in these times. One can nowadays navigate through some semblance of an Eton world such as Powell's, but it has shrunk drastically. How much is really left of Old Eton?

I pose this question over tea in an abandoned White's Club, before empty hat racks and the serried ranks of eighteenth-century worthies. My interlocutor is a London editor, a Catholic and an Etonian with a son at Eton, a man whose mild manner cannot long leave one in any doubt about either his intelligence or his ruthlessness. 'There is one thing I hate about Eton,' he starts by saying. 'This is the wretched aspect of the cult of the school, and the way in which some people never appear to get over having been there – the books they keep, full of useless memorabilia. Eton is worse in this respect than other private schools.'

He seems unsure whether to be relieved that the school's reach has diminished. The modern-day normality of the school bothers him – the way in which its rituals have been watered down, for instance. 'I am annoyed by the degree to which Old Etonians are picked on in the tabloids – because it is stupid, and because it isn't fair anyhow,' he says. 'The school has changed because there are far fewer Old Etonians' sons at school. The father of a friend of my son is an airline pilot. And one notices the foreigners at Eton. However, press coverage treats the school as if it were still exclusively populated by toffs.' We contrast the British system with the French one, even the old Soviet one. He believes that Britain is fortunate never to have acquired an elite system of lycées and Grandes Écoles. 'Britain never decided to have an elite, and Eton never really existed to form one,' he says. 'That has been its great strength –

Spottiswoode's Window where notices are posted daily, 1937

countries shouldn't just set out to have elites, should they?'

I tell him about Sampson's observation, and how Etonians are so good at politics. Why is this so? 'They are so good because it is just one of the things they do. They *choose* to go into politics, unlike the members of the French elite, in whom the notion is instilled that they must somehow belong in public life.' My interlocutor welcomes the relative lack of presence of Etonians in contemporary public life, looking forward to a time when being an Old Etonian will be rather like being Jewish – Etonians will compensate vigorously for what might appear to be a handicap. Together, we go through the existing Etonians on or near the front bench of the Tory party. He thinks that both the *Spectator* editor Boris Johnson (at that moment, shortly before his sacking for over-hastily disavowing an affair, a spokesman for Culture) and Oliver Letwin (then the Shadow Chancellor) have adequately compensated for being Etonians. Both of them, it seems, contrive a variant of the duffer act laid on by Sir Alec with his matches, but with greater skill.

As it happens I have interviewed Letwin, and he seems to me to be a truly intelligent man – someone with something not stale to say amid the wreckage of the post-Thatcher Tory party. But he also appears a parody of a country gentleman, eager to camouflage his intelligence. His ideas are rarely discussed in detail. Instead newspaper profiles refer to his 'fluting, patrician voice' or his scuffed brogues. Letwin is at pains always to be seen wearing the right overcoat. It's too easy to turn him into a 'character'. Reporters marvel that his grandparents were from Eastern Europe, and his parents American – of course they mean to say that he is Jewish and a toff – and this is deemed noteworthy. If he wasn't an Etonian, they wouldn't bother with such things.

I once heard the journalist Emma Soames (granddaughter of Sir Winston Churchill) complain that it was so hard for her Etonian brothers, brought up to imagine that everything was theirs, to adapt to classlessness. She said this with no sense of irony – but, when I saw her brother defend our military in true Tory style, utterly at ease in the House of Commons, it struck me that her anxiety might be premature because there was, as yet, no need to adapt.

Etonians did get on, although they were in a variety of small ways made to pay for it. A film I once made about neo-fascism and race hate in Europe was criticised in a gossip column of the *Daily Mail,* on the grounds that I was an Old Etonian. The idea appeared to be that Etonians shouldn't worry their heads with such issues. At dinner a London publishing executive explained to me that she had decided not to enter her son for Eton after reading the piece. 'I didn't want him to have so much baggage,' she explained crisply. 'Marlborough seemed a better bet.'

In the old days, Eton's place at the top of the system afforded some sort of protection – being so conspicuous, part of so many things, it could be said to stand clearly for something other than wealth. It did appear that the school returned something to society, as, according to the received wisdom of the day, such places were supposed to do. So the vulgar question of what Eton was for was asked only rarely.

As the Head Master had reminded me, however, Eton is now a four letter word. Many of those who write about Eton, earning journalists' salaries, cannot afford to send their children there, and, without quite admitting this, resent it. The very existence of Eton touches a contemporary core of envy or disaffection. Of course we needed some fence against the power of money, most people would admit that some vestige of a ruling elite, democratically chosen, would prove useful to us. But Eton in this role? With its royal toffs and costumes and its air of snobbery, Eton wasn't the right place. Much safer, and easier, was jeering. And one could be sure that Eton would never answer back.

One recourse adopted by Etonians today is to adopt the style of meritocracy with such assiduity that they appear indistinguishable from competitors. This is the Widmerpool option. I catch a whiff of this strategy in an Oxford drawing-room, when I talk to Michael Beloff, Q.C. and president of Trinity College. Dressed informally in a fleece and casual trousers rather than the suit he would have worn only a few years ago, an intimate of Cherie and Tony Blair, Beloff combines democratic manners with a high valuation of intelligence, not least his own. He confesses to having loved Eton immensely as a Colleger. Though he won many prizes, he tells me that he experienced regret for many years about the ones he didn't win. Here is a modern version of an old-style Etonian intellectual grandee in the old style. Beloff has become the principal spokesman in Britain of purely academic standards as a means of selecting candidates for university. He is proud of having messed with Derek Parfitt, now a professional philosopher, with Edward Mortimer, fellow of All Souls and *Times* leader writer, currently writing Kofi Annan's speeches; and Francis Cripps, 'the man who took the best First at Cambridge in economics since the war.' Beloff thinks of Eton as a model of selection in education – proof not that the slow can ever be rescued, but that the bright feed off each other, to their mutual and exclusive benefit. 'I don't meet so many Etonians in my line of business,' he says silkily. 'But I do know many people whose sons are at Eton. And that seems like progress of sorts.' Beloff recalls being taught by Mr. Parry whom he describes, perhaps a bit patronisingly, as 'not quite a Mr. Chips'. I ask whether he ever felt stressed at Eton; and Beloff replies that he didn't. 'Oh no, I loved it all so much,' he says. 'I used to want to arrive back early at the beginning of each term – just to get more of the place.'

I begin to notice many less successful forms of self-adaptation among individual Etonians. They appear to have become more thin-skinned, less overtly confident. Silent self-confidence is giving way to half-panicky admissions of failure. In the 1965 *Chronicle,* I find a piece Patrick and I commissioned from Edward Mortimer. Even then, he was able to identify the problems of being Etonian:

> I cannot condemn it without condemning myself. Alright then, I do condemn myself. I recognise myself as a member the contemporary British elite, a privileged group based on a mixture of inherited money and inherited contacts, and inherited brains… those on the outside may be expected to resent this set-up; some of them do. Those on the inside may be expected to feel guilty; some of them do, and I am one. I want to be resented; I look forward to the guillotine and my eventual release. Am I sorry I was at Eton? Nothing so simple: I am glad and I resent being glad. I even enjoy being an Old Etonian, but I dislike enjoying it. Illogical? *Sentio et excrucior.*

***

I endure many meetings in which the Etonians I contact recapitulate sporting or academic triumphs, or ask me if I knew other Etonians. But I also notice a note of anxiety creeping into interviews. Some of those whom I approach (they may have sent their sons to Eton, and now complain about how idle or spoilt they have turned out) brush away enquiry. 'Oh, the place is ridiculous,' they retort. My old Trotskyist friend, busy installing financial control systems for the Mozambique government, emails back to the effect that he cannot remember learning anything important at Eton. Another Etonian encountered at a dinner is near-speechless. His father loved the place (home life filled with trophies etc.) and he hated it. 'It's an evil institution', he informs me, loudly enough to cause a stir among the guests. 'You suffer if you don't get good enough results – which means that you suffer if you don't conform.'

Some years ago, in an effort to make money, I was briefly part of a bid for a television franchise financed by an Etonian friend – an aristocrat with connections to the Spencer family. William stammered, he wore loud pink ties, wide pinstripes, often stained; and was invariably late, and in a hurry, about to shed or put on articles of clothing from which he appeared always to be bursting out. In the nicest way, one was bound to think of him as an amateur as well as a gentleman. I was prepared for the half-crooked knees that greeted our visits to prospective investors. But I wasn't ready for so much denigration – our aristo, it was made clear, would be taken seriously only if he was prepared to detach himself from the project for which he had supplied the money. 'They want me to be a head waiter,' he explained as we went from one meeting to another. After one investor had appeared conspicuously relieved that he didn't want to be executive Chairman of the new company, William said testily to me: 'I'm really not a bad head waiter. It's not what I like to do, but I'll do it.'

When I have lunch with him years later, the bitterness is still more evident. 'No-one remembers that I was educated at Oxford, no-one wants to know that I acquired an M.B.A. at Harvard,' he tells me 'They just wish to be absolutely certain that I conform to their own unflattering view of what an Etonian should be.' To make things worse, William hated being at Eton. 'I don't want to talk about it,' he says repeatedly, and, inevitably, he does, telling me that he was fat, that he was teased for his stammer, and that he started most days in tears. Two Eton friends killed themselves in their mid-twenties, and he is sure that this wasn't a coincidence.

'In other schools you go to learn something,' he says. 'Eton is all about the boy culture. And the boy culture was no good for me – because, judged by those standards, I was never, never going to amount to anything, and I would always fail. What the school taught me was to think of myself as nothing.' Later, he says that it was alright for me – I was successful, after all, I was considered to have promise. When we part, I think of what it must mean to be always identified with what you hate most, never able to escape, or do much about it. It must indeed be like being born into the wrong caste. No wonder so many Etonians went mad, took refuge in the colonies, or stained their ties. Well into middle age, my aristo friend is about to acquire an heir; and I ask him whether he would consider sending a son to Eton. 'Not a chance,' he says, waving goodbye. 'Not a blooming chance.'

***

In between visits to Eton, I took the train to Abingdon, going by taxi to the John Mason School, a comprehensive with only slightly fewer pupils than Eton built in 1960s-style brick, to which a number of extensions appeared rapidly to have been added, pell mell, without much fore-thought or aesthetic awareness. I hadn't ever set foot inside a state school; and I was forced quickly to compare my own lavish education with the more rudimentary experience on offer here. The pupils were lively and uninhibited, plastered with gel. Many ethnic origins were represented despite the relative whiteness of Abingdon. Here one rushed from class to class, rather than strolling. The food appeared distinctly superior to its Eton equivalent. At the staff daily meeting, conversation turned to knife attacks and security.

But I am here to see Head Teacher Jeremy, among my

best friends from Eton and university. Jeremy became a teacher, I recall, through idealistic motives, in the 1970s. As we sit in his cramped office he describes long efforts to 'de-Etonianise' himself. 'I had to work on my accent,' he tells me. 'I had to find a different way of talking to people.' I remark that I cannot tell whether he had been successful in this – because he seems much the same to me. But I can understand that changing himself was a motive in life, and that it explains his presence here. He refused offers from private schools, higher pay notwithstanding. No doubt principle came into these refusals, but stubbornness was important, too – he wanted to show that he was prepared to be consistent. He tells me that his own school, highly thought of locally, is allocated £2,300 for each pupil – around one tenth of the money spent on each pupil at Eton. 'The worst thing about the state system is never having enough money to do what you want,' he says. 'It's not that we are poor – certainly not by the standards of the rest of the world – but a little more money, nothing on the Eton scale, would help us do so much more. And I can't really accept that this should be so. It does make me angry.'

This is said not with bitterness, but simply to tell me how things are. It is revealing to me that Jeremy decided never to go back to Eton, despite its proximity. 'I just can't go, although I've thought about it many times,' he says.

'Something stops me from going there, as if I might find some part of myself I have anyhow abandoned.' We talk about his children, who attended state schools, and went to university. 'I could have given them the education I had,' he says. 'But I decided not to. I thought it would be better if they didn't have it.' When I ask him if he still feels the same way, he nods – and I sense how ridiculous it remains that he should have been obliged to pay any price for what, so uncontroversially, he believes. Perhaps Jeremy did act out of a sense of scruple that might in other circumstances not have seemed appropriate – but if he hadn't, he wouldn't be running this school. I recall what the Eton Head Master (whom my friend resembles in so many ways, both physically, and in the way he talks, not to mention the very modern way of imposing discipline which they share) said about *noblesse oblige*. Jeremy still believes in *noblesse oblige*.

***

Without knowing why, I was nervous about meeting my co-editor Patrick. This was because of my memories of his own high standards. I was certain that the meeting wouldn't be cosy, perhaps forcing me into an accounting of what I had or hadn't done with my life. But my nervousness also came from the rumours that I had encountered of his own personal disasters. When we finally meet for dinner with some friends in a North Oxford restaurant, Patrick arrives late, appearing harried – maybe he, too, was nervous. Age hasn't quelled his love of gesture, and he pushes a glass of wine away so that we can all see him do this.

We plunge into the past without second thought. 'I call it the other country,' he exclaims about Eton in his familiar, thundering orator's voice; but suddenly he decides to leave school memories for later. Instead he tells us that he lived on vodka until three years ago, when he was finally carted off to hospital. Only his family saved him from what doctors thought was the prospect of imminent death – and it doesn't sound as if he is exaggerating. With the vodka, however, and, as a consequence of an ill-advised liaison with a student who reported him to the authorities, Patrick's professorship went out of the window. He's now in early retirement, lecturing and teaching a bit while he writes, a polemicist who fires off letters to the *Times* or the *London Review of Books* (alone among the British intelligentsia, he defends both Tony Blair and the hapless Lord Hutton for their role in the Iraq war and its aftermath), writing brilliantly angry essays about New Labour's disregard for humanities in the vein in which he once attacked Eton. Yet again I think of him as a pioneer – disillusioned, uncrusty, wandering the trackless paths of doubt. But this turns out to be a comprehensive misunderstanding of the ordeal which Patrick's life has been.

Patrick wants to re-initiate our collaboration – he says that our *Chronicle* was one of the best things he did. 'It was so subversive,' he says with satisfaction. 'Can't we do more together?' As the evening wears on, however, I realise that something deeper is wrong. Patrick's anguish is ravenous, all-consuming. We drive around Oxford in the rain.

'I failed,' he says to me, but not melodramatically, as if he has considered the question for many years, coming to a conclusion as one might about a historical subject.

'No', I say, 'You didn't. Why worry about something like a lost professorship?'

Sitting in the darkness of the parked car, Patrick becomes wilder and wilder. He says he made a mess of everything except his children, and he talks about religion. 'It's not what you'd think,' he says. 'There's nothing happy about what I believe in. Everything is darker than anything you would know about, filled with original sin.' The conversation turns to Eton, 'that place', as he now begins to call it. No, he couldn't blame everything on Eton – his domineering father, and other things, which he won't, or cannot specify, are equally significant. Or perhaps nothing, or no-one is to blame. But it was at Eton, just as he began to be successful, piling up prizes and scholarships, gaining confidence, that he first acquired the conviction that he would never win, and that, no matter how hard he strove, he would always feel in some way deficient. 'The problem isn't so much competitiveness,' he says sadly. 'It's something else – I always feel discontented, and I cannot get rid of it.' He pauses. 'I will die if I drink again,' he says. 'The doctors describe my alcoholism as an addiction. But I sense that that the addiction is part of the despair. That's why it's so hard to conquer it.'

***

I exchange emails with Patrick, but just before we are to meet again, I learn that he started to drink again, and died. On a rainy Oxford day I attend a very long Catholic service, held in an ugly modern chapel, packed with Patrick's friends and colleagues. His grief-stricken ex-wife tells us that she had lost Patrick many years ago. 'I can't mourn for you now,' she says, striking the wood of the coffin so that it appears to echo. She wants him to rest now, after his torments. A priest appears to leave half-open the question of whether Patrick decided to kill himself, and this seems not just tactful, but, under the circumstances, reasonable.

At a wake held in the surroundings of All Souls College,

of which Patrick was once a Fellow, I learn that he wrote what is acknowledged to be one of the most important books about the origins of law in Anglo-Saxon England. Never hostile to Europe, always looking for parallels in other countries, it appears that Patrick prized Anglo-Saxon identity. Establishing that what awaited the Normans here in England was a highly developed set of codes, in many respects superior to theirs, Patrick redefined our notions of how the English legal system was created.

I also meet old school friends wearing O.E. ties. One of them, a doctor at an East London hospital, with whom I used to go to French movies in Oxford Street, tells me he is wearing the tie on Patrick's behalf. 'I felt I had to establish my reason for being here,' he says. I ask him if he sees other Etonians, and he says that he does, but not too often. 'A surprising proportion of us are normal people, who have never amounted to anything in particular,' he says, choosing his words with great care.

CHAPTER SEVEN

The earliest intimations of public school mortality occurred in the midst of the Second World War, when the postwar New Jerusalem was still a gleam in the planners' eye. 'There is something to be said for preserving some schools only loosely connected with the national educational system...(if) their existence is favourable to initiative, experiment and the diversity of educational type,' wrote the Labour sociologist R.H. Tawney. 'There is nothing whatever to be said for preserving schools whose distinctive characteristic is that they are recruited almost exclusively from the children of parents with larger incomes than their neighbours.'

In 1943 Maynard Keynes took time off from his efforts to create global financial order in order to rescue Eton's finances – despite suffering from the heart disease that ultimately killed him, he spent a week each month in damp rooms arguing about Eton's investment strategies. Although Keynes loved being at Eton, and regarded it as a place which had influenced him greatly, by 1945 it would appear that Keynes, too, had caught the New Jerusalem bug – he now believed that the idea of an elite in Britain could only be preserved if institutions such as Eton were democratised, opening themselves up to the bright and the less rich. Perhaps, he concluded, it was time for the state to contribute to the fees of places like Eton. This would allow children to bypass private preparatory schools, going directly from primary school to a new, reformed system of state-supported, private schooling.

This eminently practical solution of Keynes (a similar compromise was shortly applied to the funding of universities) foundered on the reluctance of both parties – state schools, who didn't want to lose their pupils, as well as the excessively conservative public schools – to contemplate genuine change. In time, a few boys from the state system came to Eton, but not many. (They were known as 'Fleming Boys', after the commission that recommended that they should be admitted, and later as 'Hertfordshire boys', because the Hertfordshire educational authorities, not the local Berkshire one, entered into an arrangement with

Eton.) Contemporaries such as Jonathan Aitken remember that life wasn't easy for them. 'They never fitted in, really,' he says. Labour interest in reforming public schools was at best lukewarm and fitful. Reformers were not helped by the attitudes of the ex-trade unionist Foreign Secretary, Ernest Bevin. As a poor young man, Bevin had complained bitterly about the inequalities of British education; but many of those he now relied on at the Foreign Office were Eton-educated; and he came to admire the school ethos. 'We must never change any of this,' he told the headmaster and a group of boys assembled in School Yard, after delivering a lecture about the Cold War.

It is significant that the worst mid-century row over entry to Eton took place not in relation to grammar school boys, but foreigners, and, most specifically, Jews. It occurred because a friend of the philosopher Freddie Ayer discovered that she was unable to secure a scholarship for her son because the fathers of Collegers were required to be British. Ayer knew that the statute hadn't been in place when he was admitted to College – it would have prevented him going to Eton – and he resolved to make trouble. He became more adamant when the Provost blandly explained that Eton was worried by the 'early-development' or 'over-maturity' of 'sons of Southern Europeans and Middle Easterners,' suggesting that foreigners should be made to wait for two generations before their children were admitted. Ayer prevailed over the Provost and Fellows only after meeting Etonian minister Edward Boyle on a train, and after Boyle had raised the matter with Etonian Prime Minister, Harold Macmillan. Ayer had hated Eton, and he found his negative feelings much enhanced. 'I have enormous contempt for people with no public courage,' he said.

By the 1960s, many believed that the present system was no longer defensible. Patrick wasn't alone in his belief that Eton was doomed, and should be forthwith incorporated within the state system. 'There's no argument about it,' he would say in our impromptu editorial meetings. 'Why can't Eton be made into a direct grant school? There's nothing wrong with coming from a meritocratic elite. Isn't that the way you'd like to think of yourself?'

Within Eton it presumably seemed best to do little, and to do that as late as possible in the hope (fully justified, as it turned out) that the winds of egalitarianism would ultimately blow themselves out. The Provost and Fellows did consider relocating to Ireland or France, but this was never a very serious notion. Instead, prodded once again by Edward Boyle (by now a reforming Minister for Education who was pursuing dreams of greater equality) they began to talk of the school as being 'comprehensive'. The 1960s Labour government appeared belligerent about public school education, while lacking the nerve to do anything about it. Another report was commissioned, and those who came to Eton in order to investigate and make recommendations were duly charmed. The economist John Vaizey described Eton as 'the only good school I have ever seen.' The leftish novelist and polemicist C.P. ('Two Cultures') Snow was so impressed by the school that he decided to send his sons there. Quizzed by journalists about this, he explained that going to Eton would help his sons to know the people they were likely to meet in later life. Labour M.P. (and Etonian) Tam Dalyell, who sat on the Commons committee for education throughout the 1960s, recalled that the idea of 'doing anything' about Eton was never seriously discussed. 'It was all about money,' Dalyell told me over lunch at the House of Commons. 'Money and inconvenience. No-one wanted to do anything. Nothing was ever going to happen.'

Was it ever possible to alter the status of Eton? This is the question I want to ask Michael McCrum. He was put in to clean Eton up after the Chummy disaster, and was Head Master from 1970 to 1980. Although many whom he taught found him stiff ('stiff isn't the word, as if he had a broomstick in his trousers' is one recollection of his classes in Mediaeval Italian), others say he was probably the best Head Master Eton ever had. So I travel to Cambridge, where I'm entertained for two hours by a neat, tall man with exquisite manners, and the sort of steely, half-tolerant demeanour displayed by the best teachers. McCrum's relative indifference to worldly things is apparent from his small, donnishly book-lined study. He isn't a snob, and he has no special respect for pupils who became great and good. ('Lots of good ideas, but never quite developed,' is how he refers to Oliver Letwin.) It was McCrum who abolished beating at Eton, and who finally abolished fagging. (He failed, however, to interest Eton in the possibility of an adjacent girl's school; and his idea that Etonians might be induced to become policemen, rising through the ranks to become über-Bobbies, proved to be a flop.) 'Reforms took so much time at Eton,' he tells me. 'One had to bring along the Provost and Vice-Provost, and also the boys, who were not always keen on change, I was obliged, because it appeared more urgent, to focus instead on modernising the curriculum. I wanted to create a great school.'

McCrum tells me about his own campaign to introduce the principle of educational vouchers in Britain, and it is clear that he cares passionately about the existence of inequality. As we talk, however, I'm aware of what appears to be a persistent syndrome, evident both in the character of Eton and, in a more generalised way, throughout British life. Here is someone whom I would have been proud to have as a teacher. Here is a true radical – someone who, throughout his life, nursed many ideas about how the educational system might be improved, many of them sensible ones. At Eton, however, his radical ideas ended nowhere. He couldn't voice them until he had left – by which time he was, of course, no longer in a position to think of implementing them. 'In some respects I really did feel that I had failed,' he says candidly. In the 1970s, once again, the state system was partly to blame, never whole-heartedly encouraging its best pupils to apply. But the Provost and Fellows weren't excessively enthusiastic, nor, self-evidently, was there any pressure for change from parents. 'I was up against so much accumulated weight,' he says. 'I could run the school better, but only if I was very careful about not making changes that might in any way prove unpopular.'

Was there a moment at which, as Patrick believed, the school might have been incorporated within a national state system? It seemed not. No government wanted to incur the expense of taking on so redoubtable an opponent as Eton. Perhaps no-one cared enough. But the moment was ended by the decision to abolish grammar schools. Super-elite places like Eton or Winchester had no place in a genuinely comprehensive system – they were henceforth left to their own definitions of private excellence. I thought sadly of

Patrick's view of the failure of education in Britain, and new Labour. 'Don't you think the public schools have been terrible for Britain?' is how David Cornwell posed the question. He meant that they had been, and still were, a barrier to equality, dragging against modernisation. It was a proposition that I had heard voiced often – only to discover that many of its most vigorous proponents had elected to send their children to one or other of them. I too, had been happy to send my daughter to a private school. I believed that it was good to pile up prizes, fine to do well. I found the idea of elites unexceptionable. My own aversion to the Eton system was simpler than Patrick's, closer to McCrumb's – it wasn't the consequence of utopian visions, or even based on indignation. It was the unfairness that appeared abhorrent to me. I couldn't see why elite membership shouldn't be open to all. Why must social status and the idea of an elite come so jumbled up in Britain?

***

By the 1960s no-one would have bet on the future of Eton, and yet the place seems still to be flourishing. In appearance at least, the progressive expectations of that time have been frustrated. And yet surely this is too simple an account of things, leaving out such issues as the disappearance of deference, indeed of most traditional class attitudes. I wondered whether the pre-eminence of Eton, and schools like it, isn't in many respects delusory. They appear to be grand and rich, stuffed with money, and so indeed they are. But many of their original functions have fallen away. It would no longer be possible to return to a world in which Eton appeared to dominate so much of Britain or indeed was taken so seriously.

One indicator of change is the tone with which arguments over the future of places like Eton are conducted. In early 2005 the case of Ms. Sarah Forsyth vs. Eton College was heard at the Reading Employment tribunal, and it proved to be literate entertainment, at least as fascinating as a Rattigan play put on by staff and students. Ms. Forsyth was an arts teacher who had been dismissed by Eton. She produced tape-recordings purporting to show that Prince Harry had been helped to cheat in his 'expressive art' exams. Eton for its part responded that 'a string of spelling mistakes and grammatical errors in the text' proved that it was Harry's own work. (To the distress of those covering it, the tribunal declined to pronounce on this matter, on the grounds that it had no bearing on the case, and had already been examined elsewhere. It thus left open the question of how it was that the Prince, despite being at Eton, had managed to acquire only the minimum two A levels which allowed him to attend Sandhurst, and become an officer in the British Army.)

The case was decided in Ms. Forsyth's favour, despite criticisms that she had, unbeknownst to them, tape-recorded her employers. The judgement of Eton was harsh indeed, particularly with respect to Mr. Burke, the hapless, muddled head of the arts department, to whom the task of dismissing Miss Forsyth had fallen. The following is taken from the tribunal's judgement of the case:

There was no proper agenda or structure to that meeting [between Mr. Burke and Ms Forsyth]. Mr. Burke was disorganised in his approach. He was unprofessional in his approach. He says at the outset [of the meeting] 'Right, this will now put this on a legal footing' and further says 'I am now following government policy on how to deal with an employee.' However, the way he conducts himself indicates that he is completely unaware of how a capability interview should be conducted… "The one thing I can tell you, [Ms Forsyth], is I told you the gloves are off now. I can't protect you, because if I protect you…'

Plainly, no tradition of the 'capability interview' existed at Eton. Why should it? As for the Headmaster, Tony Little, 'whilst he accepted the need for fairness and objectivity in principle… he failed to demonstrate that in practice.' Mr. Puddefoot the Deputy Head Master was censured for being evasive. 'His perspective of events was totally "Etoncentric".'

An article in the *Guardian* by former Labour Minister, writer and defender of comprehensives Roy Hattersley told the story of Mary Gaskell Comprehensive, situated somewhere in the decayed industrial north, with 'dilapidated buildings spread over two sites.' Hattersley imagined what would have happened to the struggling head Ms. Hale (in a nice touch 'a vicar's daughter') if a similar scandal had erupted at Gaskell. 'We can predict with absolute confidence how the newspapers would react,' he said. 'The head would be excoriated as incompetent. The senior staff would be described as thugs. And the whole episode would be used as further proof that the abolition of the grammar schools was an act of wanton vandalism which could only result in an inexorable deterioration of moral as well as educational standards.' But Hattersley was wrong if he imagined that Eton's prestige would allow it to get away with such failings. He was perhaps out of date in his traditional drawing of the class war lines. It is often among those who think of themselves as middle class, paying for their children's education, that hostility to places like Eton sometimes seems most intense. This may be (as defenders of the system insist) a question of resentment at the wealth of others. But resentment is also rooted in the newly acquired perception in Britain that all class distinctions are a racket. Eton, in common with the aristocracy and the royal Family, has had longer, and more leisure, in which to learn how these distinctions may be sustained. It has learnt to play the class game.

***

Contradictory, shifting attitudes to class are also on display when it comes to the question of whether Etonians should become leaders of the Tory party. Ten years ago the stiff, crimped-hair patrician Douglas Hurd was felled in his Tory leadership bid by the newscaster Jon Snow. 'You went to to Eton, for heaven's sake,' Snow exclaimed, thus dismissing him. Hurd, for his part seemed genuinely surprised by the degree of hostility aroused by his Eton past. 'I was brought up on a farm,' he said. 'This is inverted snobbery. I thought I was running for leader of the Tory party, not some demented Marxist sect.' Barracking Etonian speakers in the House of Commons continued to be a popular sport. When David Cameron's candidacy first appeared a possibility, Jon Snow aksed the same question of Oliver Letwin as he had of Hurd, 'Could an Etonian really run the Tory party?' 'It is a disadvantage for the job,' Letwin replied, plainly annoyed by the question. 'But it doesn't matter anyhow.'

Newspapers like the *Times* suggested that 'Etonian David Cameron' might be a suitable Tory leader – but only if he called himself Dave, promoting himself as a "Skoda-driving sports fan who loves the Smiths," and discarding his 'faintly patrician air'. Even the *Spectator* asked 'Can the Tories choose a Toff?' An article touting Cameron conceded the obvious – the school had 'become disadvantageous for Conservative politicians'. 'It's still kind of fabulous for the sons of London hairdressers and senior PRs holding luxury brand portfolios,' gushed Vicki Woods.

Cameron cannily deflected discussion of his education with the bland, unexceptionable remarks that rapidly became his trademark. ('It's not where you come from that matters, it's where you're going,' he said in his unscripted Blackpool speech, to rapturous blue-rinse applause.) He may even have been helped in his efforts by his apparently unwise decision to discuss his attitude to drugs. It wasn't clear whether his success signalled a long overdue shift in attitudes; or whether it merely delivered the message that Etonians like Cameron ('posh' and 'nice' were the adjectives affixed to him) have become men adept at circumnavigating the reefs of class war.

'I've never met an Etonian who actually said he wanted

to be a cabinet minister,' a beak told me. 'Of course Etonians are deeply political, in the sense that they want to be rich and influential. But that means something different now. It's just not cool to be overtly political.' Cameron wasn't active, or it would seem, much interested in politics, either at Eton or, later, at Oxford. Despite being a professional (he had worked for the Tories before running the PR side of a television company), he appeared enough of an outsider to seem fresh. In a contemporary context (especially for a Tory party grown desperate and old, which regarded the baby-faced Cameron, perhaps a bit misleadingly, as the incarnation of Tory youth) he didn't appear to be a party hack. Bizarrely, the Eton Thing probably helped him – because Etonians, so long identified with the exercise of power had, for the moment at least, acquired the glamour of outsiders.

There were those who praised the right wing tone of many of Cameron's formulations; but, as any Etonian knew, this was likely to prove an illusion. Etonians were the ultimate pragmatists. 'I'm not a deeply ideological person; I'm a practical one,' Cameron told the *Observer*, and he was surely being truthful. Like his predecessor, he would cut deals, make compromises and, once in power, even tell half-truths, all the while talking of public service. But one could also be certain that Cameron would never return to the appearance of the old Eton-style government by cabal.

***

An Eton devoid of its connection to power was until recently unimaginable, and so, too, was an Eton that didn't send a large a proportion of its sons to Oxford and Cambridge. But what would happen if Eton was severed from these roots?

At Eton, happily, consideration of such a prospect can be put off for a rainy day. 'It's like playing for Manchester United rather than Wrexham,' is how a young German master describes the transition from the state system to Eton. He is talking about everything that makes each boy seem special. Why bow to educational fashions? The school shells out around £2.3 million each year in scholarships and in subsidies to summer schools. It has been able to construct a rowing lake capable of being used for Olympic training. (The lake can be used by the public, or by rowing associations, but on a significant number of afternoons, in winter as well as summer, it is reserved for Etonians.) Leaving aside its buildings, which are deemed priceless, and its £30 million Gutenberg Bible, the school possesses assets of around £160 million. These make Eton a rich place – though they pale beside the size of American educational endowments. But the Provost and Fellows argue that Eton needs to be still richer in order to be more effectively beneficent. They would like to see Etonians donate another £100 million. This would 'refresh the school's finances'. And would allow any boy selected to be given a place, no matter what his origins. In theory, therefore, the school would thus return to its own identity and its past – a place for rich boys, though brighter now, and poorer ones, too.

Is Eton really threatened by the spectre of an egalitarian, levelling government? I don't think so. The guarantee of freedom in education (a protection given first to Catholic schools throughout Europe, then extended, as a principle of democracy) means that the possibility of state coercion no longer exists. Haters of privilege can only strive to make life more difficult. Within this category of hostility falls a recent, somewhat perfunctory investigation into price-fixing, in which both Eton and Winchester were implicated.*

More serious is the prospective removal of the charitable status which has long vexed Labour activists. As a charity, Eton saves at least £1 million a year. If it loses its status, becoming a business, the school might be obliged either to

*In February 2006, 50 public schools, including Eton, Harrow, Winchester and Wesminster were fined a total of £3.5 million in a deal struck with the Office of Fair Trading. A fine of £10,000 was levied from each school; around £50,000 was placed in trust for those pupils who might have been overcharged. These sums, according to the *Times*, were far below the sums the OFT could have levied.

offer fewer services (not a desirable outcome where rich parents are involved) or make being at Eton still more expensive. A problem of Eton is just how expensive it is starting to become. In relation to 1970, fees have more than doubled in real terms. As the bursar concedes, 'the school is becoming far more expensive than we would wish.'

The not-so-affluent middle-classes are already being priced out. A discreetly titled 'application for school fee assistance' sent to applicants by the Bursar covers twenty-odd pages. In the style of a new Domesday Book, parents

Boys buying buttonholes, 1907

are asked whether they or their forebears went to Eton. They are required to state, in addition to their income, the acreage of their property and the year of their car. 'Do you have any other capital assets (e.g. works of art, vintage car, silver, etc.)?', it asks. It also asks what proportion of the £23,000 fees parents can afford. Henry VI decreed that all scholars should be paid for in full, but nowadays only a small number of boys pay nothing at all. 248 boys, or around nineteen per cent of the school, receive some sort of assistance. Through bursaries, music scholarships etc., the school will pay up to 50 per cent of the fees, leaving parents to stump up the equivalent of the cost of a middling to posh London day school. As for the school's euphemistically titled Junior scholarships – its plan to 'take four boys out of state school each year and educate them until they are eighteen' – this hasn't been successful. Last year only 50 parents applied, and one year no scholarships at all were awarded. 'The difficulty we find is in encouraging people to have a go,' admits the master in charge of the scheme.

Eton has always fancied social exotics, lumping them with princelings as an alternative to creeping middle classdom. But the school is not able or willing to contemplate ambitious social engineering outside its own, strictly limited turf – it has never been required to do this, after all.

How many of those attending Eton on scholarships come from genuinely poor backgrounds? Although the Head Master cites a boy from a tower block, this would seem no more than a gesture. It would be safe to conclude that many recipients of assistance are relatively prosperous, coming from today's version of what Orwell, alluding to his own family, called 'the lower upper class' – no longer army types, perhaps, but less affluent professionals, even journalists. In this respect Eton has remained surprisingly true to its traditions.

But if the school is not threatened by abolition, or absorption, it is under pressure as a consequence of the Labour government's (and many university dons') desire to favour those from the state education system. Only universities willing to comply with 'targets' – i.e. that take more children from state schools – are to be favoured with extra funds. This is a policy that has been criticised for its lack of practicability; but its motives are not ideological. It is a hard-headed way of favouring one lump of the large British middle class over another, rewarding those who choose to send their offspring to state schools rather than relying on private ones. It is also a means of removing another middle class subsidy – itself a form of social engineering, as it is argued. Pursued zealously, the policy poses a serious threat to places like Eton.

There is nothing new about the odd don taking a dislike to Etonians. The writer Adam Nicolson recalls going for an interview in the late 1970s at King's College, Cambridge wearing his best gray double-breasted suit and Turnbull and Asser shirt. 'I was confronted by this radical English don wearing sneakers and shades, with his legs sideways over a leather chair. "Why do you think the government should pay you to read poetry for three years?" he asked.' When Nicolson muttered 'something about civilisation consisting of the obligation, or the right to read poetry,' the don snorted. But Nicolson's Eton beak was able to call a friend in another college, getting his pupil accepted. 'The man who took me later said: "If I am asked to choose between a man who can do his sums and a good man, I'll always choose the good man." And that's how you got into university in those days.'

But it would appear that things are somewhat different now. 'The school is in denial about its problems,' a young Etonian tells me. 'Many dons at Oxford and Cambridge don't want Etonians. It's so obvious that you are not welcome. That's pretty much what they tell you when you go for an interview – sometimes they show you what they feel by leaving you kicking your heels for hours while they interview other candidates. They don't treat boys from other public schools in this way, only Etonians. Of course the

211

school says that around 80 boys go there each year. But this doesn't take account of how much better the school has become. It should be sending even more pupils to good universities.' An Eton education must be a ticket to university. This is what parents are now paying for – not the clothes, the royal or aristocratic connections, not the contacts in later life. If the school fails to deliver such previously guaranteed access, it will, slowly, to be sure, become far less attractive. Families rich enough to afford the substantial costs of an American university will be unaffected; and more are choosing to send their sons to the United States. But it would be naïve to imagine that, even at Eton, many can do this, or will want to.

***

Perhaps others will succeed where the likes of Keynes failed so conspicuously, tying Eton into the British state system by means of an eleventh-hour rapprochment, but this seems unlikely. It seems too late for such a move. The hearing at Reading is a sign that the school is ill-suited to the many small compromises implied by progressive educational bureaucracy. Another fate most surely awaits Eton, one more in keeping with the gaudy, pragmatic aspect of its traditions. Eton will successfully exploit its own brand, opening little (or larger) Etons in Canton and Thailand. Of course it will be still more tightly focused on achievement. It will become a world-talent school, part-severing its links with Britain even as it sells its history still more assiduously. Why should Eton not simply come to represent the new world elite – who are transnational, barely touched by social origins, and rich enough to pay pretty much anything? Though one may regret this, the Eton arrogance and eccentricity will surely be tamed. There will be no problem finding corporate sponsors, and for the very bright and not quite so rich, scholarships will be freely available. A brutal streak of contemporary meritocracy will finally kill off the school's long cohabitation with the titled. (There will be room for the odd British royal, though not perhaps for Harry, or indeed for Expressive Art). Dissent will be permitted, in the best Eton style. There is no reason why the George Orwell society should cease to exist. Defenders of the new Eton will say that the school was created to fulfil this destiny, and that its long interim period of furnishing a range of talents for the British elite was no more than a prelude to this new and happy state. Why should the production of gentlemen suddenly come to a halt in the 21st century?

'Remember that Eton is a luxury brand,' the editor of the *Tatler* reminds me. 'Luxury brands have come back into their own. Eton stands for high quality, grandness and confidence about yourself. English is spoken in every capital of the world, and wherever it is spoken, people have heard of Eton.' Geordie Greig is surely right. Eton's fate will be no different from the one reserved for other up-against-it cash-strapped institutions, such as Oxford and Cambridge. But Eton will go faster and more willingly, without even the semblance of a struggle, because it stakes so much on its own, highly adaptable version of worldly success. In the true English style, Eton will be transformed without anyone acknowledging that this has happened. And, of course, Eton will flourish. Will anyone still mourn the old Eton?

CHAPTER EIGHT

The Fourth of June is the day when Eton, under the guise of commemorating the birthday of mad King George III, celebrates itself. It's best to arrive early, before the narrow roads are jammed with BMWs and Range Rovers. People begin parking on Dutchman's around nine am, and they take off their jackets, putting together small, green-coloured tents and folding tables on which they place food wrapped in tin foil. Bottles of wine or champagne are extracted from their coolers and uncorked. The men wear blazers, cream or blue striped shirts, Eton Ramblers, or O.E. ties. Some of them sport Panamas, decked with some half-forgotten House ribbon. They have modest-sized paunches and the brick-red complexions still peculiar to the English upper class in successful middle age. The fruity Eton drawl is recognisable. Most mothers are dressed down, many of them with the air of having looked through a cupboard for weeks in search of something that won't stand out. Those from London are chiefly recognisable by a *soigné* hairdo, or the giveaway designer bag with a gold chain. Sisters come in radically different shapes and styles. They are leggy and angular, blond, for the most part, nervously after the more attractive boys, wearing over-large floppy hats. Or they are puffier and jolly, wearing clothes deemed suitable for their mothers. Just a few appear heart-breakingly beautiful. Etonians are smarter than usual, devoid of egg stains, with pressed creases. Other than the coloured carnations it is the different collars and buttons that one notices, some for Pop, some for the Sixth Form. There are also boys wearing white ducks, blue or green shirts with ridiculously wide stripes, and what appear to be the kind of short, dark blue majorette jackets with gold braid edges still favoured by retro rock stars. They carry boaters topped by enormous bunches of flowers – purples, magentas, blues, reds and yellows, out-landish tropical growths of green. These are periodically placed on heads, or tilted at passers-by. Plainly, these lavish-ly decorated boys are the most important people here.

Cricket starts early, and it is watched in a desultory way. A sleepy, sepia effect is created around the white figures on green. It is hard to say who is winning, and nobody appears to care very much. Around mid-morning people make their way to School Yard, thence to the long, beautiful panelled room known as Upper School, where, beneath busts of school worthies, they watch their Sixth Form sons, dressed in court jackets and black stockings, declaim pieces of prose and poetry. This year the theme is *Girls, Girls, Girls* – and these seventeen-year-olds give us, among other goodies, bits of Mrs. Thatcher (the speech on Not Turning), Queen Elizabeth addressing her troops at Tilbury; and one of the less unsuitably scabrous passages from Germaine Greer's *The Female Eunuch..* The effect is oddly touching, without being camp. Outside, the Head Master, dressed in full penguin uniform, poses for photos with boys and parents. There are small clouds in a light blue sky, and a soft Thames valley ambience envelopes the day. Parents are unaffectedly proud of their sons' performances. 'It was wonderful, darling, just wonderful,' I hear someone say to the boy who impersonated Mrs. Thatcher.

Back on Dutchman's, Pimms and wine are being consumed. Some lunches, to which up to five separate families have contributed, are very elaborate. Others consist of sausage rolls, coronation chicken and smoked salmon. All the habitual Eton business of exchanging contacts occurs; someone asks about holidays in France. If there is talk of school, or exam results, it is of the most approving sort. It would be hard in this context to imagine any complaints, any grievances, anything indeed to disturb the equable flow of contentment.

The high moment of the day begins with another leisurely exodus, this time in the direction of Fellow's Eyot and the shaded river. On the bank, within a series of enclosures, school and parents assemble. There are printed programmes, and the Head Master is in attendance. As the boats arrive, a band strikes up. Of course, the 'Boating Song' is played, and the serial waltz-time silliness of the music echoes over the water:

Jolly boating weather
And a hay harvest breeze
Blade on the feather
Shade off the trees

By tradition the ten man Monarch rows straight past, without fanfare. Other boats come more or less gracefully to a halt while the rowers raise their oars two by two and, laboriously, appearing to take forever, sometimes seeming about to founder, get to their feet:

Rugby may be more clever,
Harrow may make more row,

But we'll row for ever
Steady from stroke to bow

It takes a very long time for the ten boats to perform this simple manoeuvre. Until recently, the procession took place in the dark, and it was followed by fireworks, culminating in a display on the opposite bank, in the shape of the school lilies, fleur de lys and lion. When waggish O.E.s got themselves up as frogmen, overturning the boats, tradition gave way to convenience. The crowd stirs restlessly:

And nothing in life shall sever
The chain that is round us now.

Now it's time to think of practical things – how to separate daughters from their dates, how to get out of the car park before the crowd becomes too large. Suddenly, like a light switched off, the Eton moment is gone; and people make for home.

***

Going home in convoy, I think once again of the strangeness of Eton. Of course, I have been told that the school has changed, but I do not really think it has changed much, or

Procession of boats, Fourth of June, 1906

indeed enough. If I had a son, I would not have wanted to send him to Eton, concluding, reluctantly perhaps, that the whole racket was too much of a good thing. I would surely not have concluded that my son deserved to inherit my own passionately conflicted view of the British elite. I have been asked the same questions, over and over again, for most of my life. Did I go to Eton? Did I really go to Eton? I reply in the affirmative, politely, because Etonians are said to have good manners. A truer Etonian (a bluer, or less self-conscious one, someone whose family line wound through the school, someone who had *truly* belonged there) might be able to brush such questions to one side, but I cannot.

Eton never left me, which is the same as saying that some piece of Eton remained with me long after I left. The oddest thing was how aware I was of this burden – and how much I resented it – even as I failed to get rid of it. I once talked about my schooling to the leftish television producer and Labour M.P Philip Whitehead. 'The hardest journey for an Old Etonian is the road from Eton to Slough,' he intoned, in the mock accents of class war. My problem was that the road, far from stopping at Slough, or even at the end of the M4, appeared endless. Did one slouch elegantly along it, as if between classes, or march with forthright step? Where did one ultimately fetch up? I set out with the minimal resolve not to look back. I wouldn't be a school bore. Next came the question of what I was supposed to do. It would have been easier if I could tell myself that some special destiny awaited me, but I couldn't. I had been told I was talented so often. It didn't help that these were the 1960s, in which the entire notion of a vocation, or indeed a profession, was cast into doubt. I could always say that I was busy experimenting with my life. No-one was going to ask me what these experiments were *for*. Via familiarity with the rules of existentialist French literature, however, the feeling of inauthenticity took hold of me. Clearly, I must begin to fail at what I did – if only as a compensation for all that Eton success. I could do what I wanted so long as I allowed myself to spoil whatever I was doing. So I hit on a solution – I would start and stop things. No sooner had I started anything – a job, a book, a fresh career – than I'd find some wholly convincing grounds for dissatisfaction. Oh, it was easy – all I had to do was remind myself of so much promise in order to destroy it.

The first thing to do was consummate my relationship with the English Master. In relation to this cropped, some-what austere but not unhandsome figure, I experienced neither love, nor desire, nor any real affection – only an embarrassed wonder about whatever it was I had got myself into. I didn't even think much whether I was homosexual or bisexual – so much less-than-successful business with bra straps gave me an answer to that question. I'm not even sure if I was terribly needy. But something less than con-vincing got done in a dank Irish hotel, in between readings of W.B.Yeats and the contemplation of wet stone. I didn't really feel anything at all. Later, after I'd seen off my seducer following a not so brief (and sexless) encounter on a remote island off the coast of southern Italy, I wondered how much I had hurt him. To the list of things or people one must never trust it struck me that one must add Etonians. But I did examine myself. I looked at the way in which, confronted with their own behaviour, near-crazy, or merely destructive friends took solace from the notion that they somehow didn't know what they were doing. Of course I knew exactly what was going on.

***

One late sunlit autumn afternoon in Oxford, when I was 21, the girl who lived upstairs in my ramshackle, chic digs by the canal, called down to say my mother wanted to speak to me. I was sure what had happened before I took the receiver. Ill for some years, my father had fallen over in a City street, on the way to his office, and he had died of heart disease. I had neglected my father, never really loving him, and now I was to pay in full. As much as I felt punished, I felt relieved, too, and then guilty. But the anticlimax I experienced at Oxford rapidly fell away. I had the funeral to attend to and, when that was finished, my work, which now seemed like a kind of survival. I decided to make up for two years of half-motivation. I left Oxford with the First that I had always wanted, and the misplaced conviction that everything would be somehow alright.

I thought of Eton for many years. I took care never to

return, of course, but I wasn't prepared to deny I had been there. My American girlfriend, later my wife, spoke of my 'divine discontent' – a phrase that I found to be a ridiculous but nonetheless accurate description of my sub-Hamlet state of mind. These were the 1970s, after all, a mediocre decade in which glumness was mandated, and I was a spectacular instance of the morose. I could be viewed as overequipped and doomed – an expensive sample, as one acquaintance told me, of the soon-to-be-extinct capitalist past. But I hung onto stubbornly-held, Eton Whig-liberal notions. 'Where did you get these ideas?' people would ask. 'At aristocratic, elitist Eton', I replied, and they would snigger, happy to patronise. It would be nice to report that I wasn't affected by these exchanges, but also misleading. And yet I never quite saw myself as an item of class pathology.

What did I want? To be free, to be loved, to be myself, to be the person I'd glimpsed at Eton, and then lost. To be able to feel good about all the Eton notions of individual freedom and privilege that now appeared to be a curse. But this was proving to be difficult. I'd start things, be successful, find out that it wasn't enough – and do the same all over again. Over the years I became aware, diffidently at first, that I would finally be able to bring this post-Eton syndrome of mine to an end.

From the outside my life looked pretty much what one would expect from the young and talented and not-quite-focussed. But it felt different from where I stood – not exactly hellish, to be sure, but definitively unserene. After Oxford, I tried living in New York; I came back to London. Married two years later, I went to New York again, in search of failure. And fail I did, getting sacked from a job, free-lancing and living in a way I couldn't really afford. The Eton thing lingered on as style, of course, but, more importantly, as a sense of invulnerability, of having so many lives left, and this propelled me into greater risk. By now I truly wanted to fail. And so I did, finally, in New York. My life with the woman who was now my wife had come into existence the day I found out that my own father had died. It was only appropriate that that our own relationship should end the instant I answered the phone again, standing in the kitchen of a run down house in rural Connecticut, and found that her mother had killed herself. I suspect that neither of us was surprised. We had done almost everything we could. We knew that something like this would happen. And yet we both responded with the acknowledgement that we, too, were finished.

By the simple expedient of hiring a crooked accountant, I lost the rest of my father's not inconsiderable unwanted bequest. In a passable imitation of the *Rake's Progress*, I began to drink, heavily. Because I knew what I was doing, however, my control never wholly slipped. I must destroy myself in order finally to grow up, this I knew. Thus prepared, I'd sit in a dusty Upper West Side chair and unpack in vast, unstoppable details the events of my adolescence. My bewigged, faintly rabbinical therapist listened to these confidences with what appeared to be great interest. So I told him the lot – about the colour test, beatings, the avoiding of importunate older boys asking for blow jobs, the bra straps that wouldn't undo, and my father who wouldn't ever quite let me be. Above all, I told him what it was to want so badly to be someone, and to be trained never wholly to show it – in consequence, to live in fear of something being found out. I howled on about fraudulence. I'm not this person, I'd say, I didn't want to be him. Truly, all these years, it wasn't me. It wasn't my decision to be this sort of person – how can I be fully responsible for what I became at Eton?

One night after therapy I went to a party given by British Foreign Office people in New York, at which one of the guests was an American academic living in London who had written a much praised book about the myth of the Victorian Gentleman, entitled *Trollope: Individuality and Moral Conduct*. Though I wasn't to know this, the author was what we would now term a neo-con; and it became apparent in our conversation that she believed sternly in the usefulness of tradition as a fence against liberal anarchy – not a perspective with which I had, or indeed have any sympathy. And of course I wasn't to know that Shirley Letwin was the mother of Oliver Letwin, who had just left Eton with his own harvest of honours. But I do recall saying to Mrs. Letwin, perhaps somewhat drunkenly, that no-one should need Eton, that the label of Etonian shouldn't have been so hard to carry. I don't think I said the place was awful. These were the early days of Mrs. Thatcher's ascendancy and Mrs. Letwin, a trim, dark-haired figure in a print dress, wasn't sympathetic. I should be ashamed at turning my back on so much, she said primly. She meant I should get a grip on myself. All was for the good, class was good, and the British elite a thoroughly good thing. Hierarchies were what caused the world to function.

For the first time in my life I realised that I no longer cared about such things. I cannot recall how I left the party, or indeed how I managed to drive back to rural Connecticut, but I stayed up most of the night feeling happy. I had no marriage, and pretty much no money left. But it also seemed to me that I had no Eton. I could perhaps begin to live.

<u>O.E.s...</u>

Walpole, Sir Robert

Pitt, William

Gladstone, William Ewart

Fearnley-Whittingstall, Hugh

Macmillan, Harold

Lawson, Dominic

Douglas-Home, Sir Alec

Astor, Hon. David

al-Sabah, HH Sheikh

Mohammed al-Moubarak

Flyte, Lord Sebastian

Singh, HH Prince Frederick

Duleep

HRH Prince Harry

HRH Prince William

Aitken, Jonathan

Cameron, David

Wooster, Bertie

Canning, 1st Viscount

Hook, Captain James

Churchill, Lord Randolph

Hurd, Douglas,

Johnson, Boris

Lloyd, George, Lloyd

Waldegrave, William

Ayer, Sir Alfred

Orwell, George

Coleridge, Nicholas

Jodhpur,, Maharajah of

Fleming, Ian

Hornblower, Simon

Huxley, Aldous

Lane Fox, Robin

Kennedy, Sir Ludovic

Laurie, Hugh

Longford, Francis Lord

Moore, Charles

Mortimer, EJ

Pinsent, Sir Matthew

Walpole, Horatio

Bond, James

Dipendra of Nepal,HM

Powell, Anthony

Whitaker, Ben

Mosley, Nicholas

Shelley, Percy Bysshe

More, Henry

Sumner, John

Devonshire, William

Merton, Sir Thomas

Keynes, John Maynard

Gascoigne, Bamber

Lewis, Damian

Salisbury, Robert Cecil,

Milburn, Oliver

Lyttelton, Humphrey

Widmerpool, Kenneth

Bacon, Francis Thomas

Grenville, George

Balfour, Arthur

Weldon, John

Swinburne, Algernon

Matthew, Uncle (Lord
Alconleigh)

Townsend, Charles

Canning, George

Norwich, John Julius

Clyde, Jeremy

Wellington, 1st Duke of

Nicolson, Nigel

Jopling, Jay

North, Frederick

Frieda, Jordan

Holroyd, Michael

Wimsey, Lord Peter

Murray, John

Parker Bowles, Tom

Matthew, Uncle (Lord
Alconleigh)

Shawcross, William

Legge-Bourke, Harry

Cazenove, Christopher

Vestey, Samuel

Browning, Oscar

Dimsdale, Sir Joseph

Darcy, Mark

Curzon,George
Nathaniel

Astor, John Jacob

HRH Prince Henry of
Gloucester

Nicholas of Romania,

Goldsmith, Sir James

Connolly, Cyril

Oates, Captain

Brummel, Beau

Siam, HH Prince of

Gore-Booth, Paul,

Letwin, Oliver

The literature on Eton is copious and, by and large, enter-taining. Those seeking greater detail than I have provided should consult the official school history, *Eton Renewed*, (John Murray, 1994), and *Eton Established* (John Murray, 2001) by Tim Card, who taught mathematics at the school, becoming Vice-Provost. These books are humane, drily humorous and suprisingly frank.

Etonians have written about themselves or their school-days with verve and persistence. Among autobiographics, my own favourites are: *Enemies of Promise* by Cyril Connolly (André Deutsch, 1998); *War and Shadows* by Sir David Fraser (Penguin/Allen Lane, 2002); *The Life of My Choice* by Wilfred Thesiger (Fontana, 1988) and *Rules of the Game* by Nicholas Mosley (Dalkey Archive, 1983). A more recent account of the school is to be found in *Stand Before Your God* by Peter Watkins (Faber, 1993). *A Dance to the Music of Time*, Anthony Powell's twelve-book cycle, is help-fully reassembled in four volumes (Arrow, 2000). The real-life story of Powell's Eton days occurs in *To Keep the Bell Rolling: The Memoirs of Anthony Powell, Vol 1: Infants of the Spring* (1976).

A dazzling array of biographies awaits the additionally inquisitive. Both *Curzon*, by David Gilmour (John Murray,

1994) and *John Maynard Keynes* (3 vols. Macmillan, compressed to a single volume) are among the greatest contemporary biographical achievements. *A.J Ayer: A life* by Ben Rogers (Vintage, 2000), and *Orwell: The Life* by D.J Taylor (Chatto and Windus, 2003) give devoted accounts of their subjects and milieux. Those seeking illumination in relation to the lost political culture of Etonness and modern Toryism should consult the excellent *The Guardsman* by Simon Bell (Harper Collins, 2004), and Geoffrey Wheatcroft's entertaining *The Strange Death of Tory England* (Penguin/Allen Lane, 2005). Alan Clark's *Diaries* are a mine of Etoniana as well as giving a shrewd, funny account of the extinction of the Eton ethos during the Thatcher era, while Danny Danziger's *Eton Voices* (Viking, 1988) assembles interviews with 42 Etonians – "There is an eerie sameness about them," he concludes.

ACKNOWLEDGEMENTS

Many Etonians were interviewed for this book, and some of the material is drawn from conversations held before the book was dreamed of. This accounts for the fact that some interviewees are named, and others are not. But there are no 'composites' – all the Etonians here as real as I can make them.

I have also made use of Danny Danziger's excellent *Eton Voices,* and must thank him for his diligence. Thanks, too, to the staff of Eton College, most of all the Head Master, Tony Little, and his assistant Vicki Keppel. They probably won't agree with much in this book, but I hope they enjoy it. Kevin Pakenham read drafts of the manuscript with patience. Frederick Mocatta proved to be both a terrific latter-day guide to Eton mysteries, and an adept spotter of howlers. My thanks go to Shanida Scotland for tolerating discussion of Eton lore, and to Rebecca Nicolson, Aurea Carpenter and Vanessa Webb of Short Books; and, specially, to my family, who accepted the alien presence of Eton in their midst.

I'm A Teacher
Get Me Out of Here!
Francis Gilbert
1-904977-02-2 PAPERBACK £6.99

At last, here it is. The book that tells you the unvarnished truth about teaching. By turns hilarious, sobering, and downright horrifying, *I'm a Teacher, Get me Out of Here* contains the sort of information that you won't find in any school prospectus, government advert, or Hollywood film.

In this astonishing memoir, Francis Gilbert candidly describes the remarkable way in which he was trained to be a teacher, his terrifying first lesson and his even more frightening experiences in his first job at Truss comprehensive, one of the worst schools in the country.

Follow Gilbert on his rollercoaster journey through the world that is the English education system; encounter thuggish and charming children, terrible and brilliant teachers; learn about the sinister effects of school inspectors and the teacher's disease of 'controloholism'. Spy on what really goes on behind the closed doors of inner-city schools.

"Gilbert is a natural storyteller. I read this in one jaw-dropping gulp."
Tim Brighouse, Commissioner for London Schools, *TES*

The Good Granny Guide
Or how to be a modern grandmother
Jane Fearnley-Whittingstall
1-9040977-08-1   £12.99

As all good grandparents know, the most precious gift they can offer their grandchildren is time.

In *The Good Granny Guide*, you will find a whole range of practical advice to help you make the most of the time you spend with your grandchildren.

Jane Fearnley-Whittingstall, an enthusiastic and closely involved grandmother of four, has gathered first-hand tips from other grandparents and their families in many different situations. The result is a hugely insightful handbook – a wonderful resource of wisdom, history and humour – covering everything from childcare trouble-shooting to what NOT to say to the daughter-in-law.

"Sound on everything from nappies to tantrums.
Jane Fearnley-Whittingstall gets the golden
rules right. She is spot on."
Philip Howard

How to be a Bad Birdwatcher
To the greater glory of life
Simon Barnes
1-904977-05-7 Paperback   £7.99

Look out of the window.
See a bird.
Enjoy it.
Congratulations. You are now a bad birdwatcher.

Anyone who has ever gazed up at the sky or stared out of the window knows something about birds. In this funny, inspiring, eye-opening book, Simon Barnes paints a riveting picture of how bird-watching has framed his life and can help us all to a better understanding of our place on this planet.

How to be a bad birdwatcher shows why birdwatching is not the preserve of twitchers, but one of the simplest, cheapest and most rewarding pastimes around.

"A delightful ode to the wild world outside
the kitchen window"
Daily Telegraph